— Great Themes of the Bible —

CHRIST:

Jesus' Life, Teaching, and Ministry

Harry C. Kiely

ABINGDON PRESS
NASHVILLE

GREAT THEMES OF THE BIBLE
Christ: Jesus' Life, Teaching, and Ministry
By Harry C. Kiely

Copyright © 2004 by Abingdon Press

ISBN 0-687-03804-9

This book is printed on recycled, acid-free, and elemental-chlorine–free paper.

MANUFACTURED IN THE UNITED STATES OF AMERICA

05 06 07 08 09 10 11 12 13 14—10 9 8 7 6 5 4 3 2 1

Table of Contents

Welcome to
Great Themes of the Bible

We are pleased that you have chosen *Great Themes of the Bible* for your small-group study. This series of study books cultivates faith formation in contemporary life using reliable principles of Christian education to explore major themes of the Bible, the issues and questions generated by these themes, and how the Bible illuminates our response to them in daily life. The sessions provide many opportunities for spiritual growth through worship, study, reflection, and interaction with other participants.

Great Themes of the Bible Cultivates Faith Formation in Contemporary Life

Who is God? How is God at work in our world? How does God call us and relate to us? How do we relate to God and to one another? What does Jesus Christ reveal to us about God? What is the potential for life in which we choose to be committed to God through Jesus Christ? How do we find hope? Such questions are at the heart of faith formation in contemporary life.

The Bible presents great themes that are universally relevant for the faith formation of all human beings in all times and places. Great themes like call, creation, covenant, Christ, commitment, and community provide points of encounter between contemporary life and the times, places, and people in the Bible. As we reflect upon faith issues in our daily lives, we can engage biblical themes in order to learn more about God and in order to understand and interpret what it means to live with faith in God.

The great themes of the Bible are the great themes of life. They generate questions and issues today just as they did for those in the biblical world. As we identify and explore these themes, we also engage the related questions and issues as they emerge in our contemporary life and culture. Exploring the Bible helps us see how people in the biblical world dealt with the issues and questions generated by a particular theme. Sometimes they responded exactly the way we would respond. Other times, they responded quite differently. In every case, however, we can glimpse God at work as we compare and contrast their situations with our own.

In Christian faith formation, we delve again and again into the Bible as we reflect upon our daily lives in light of Christian teaching. One way to imagine this process is by envisioning a spiral. A theme in the Bible generates questions and issues. We reflect upon the theme and consider the questions and issues it raises in our contemporary lives. We read the Bible and ask ourselves how the stories and teachings inform the theme and its questions and issues. We reflect upon the insights we have gained and perhaps make adjustments in our lives. We spiral through a particular theme and its issues and questions more than once as we look to the Bible for help, guidance, and hope. As we participate in this ongoing process, we gain deeper awareness of who God is and what God wants us to do, to be, and to become. The books in the *Great Themes of the Bible* series are structured around this spiraling process of faith formation.

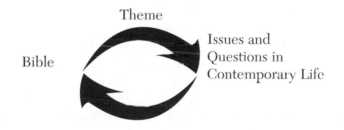

Theme

Bible

Issues and Questions in Contemporary Life

Great Themes of the Bible Is Built Upon Reliable Christian Education Principles

The sessions in each of the books in *Great Themes Of The Bible* are based on the Scriptures and lesson guides in the *Uniform Series of International Bible Lessons for Christian Teaching.* These guides provide reliable Christian education principles to those who write the books. Session development for a book in *Great Themes of the Bible* is guided by a unifying principle that illuminates the unity between life and the Bible by emphasizing a key theme. The principle contains three components: a life statement, a life question, and a biblical response.

The lesson guides in the Uniform Series also include statements for every Scripture that help the writer to think about and develop the sessions. These statements occur in five categories or matrices: Learner, Scripture, Faith Interaction, Teaching Strategies, and Special Interest.

Statements in the Learner matrix identify general characteristics describing life stages, developmental issues, and particular experiences (special needs, concerns, or celebrations) that characterize learners.

Statements in the Scripture matrix identify a variety of key issues, questions, practices, and affirmations raised from the biblical texts. These may include historical, cultural, ethical, and theological perspectives.

Statements in the Faith Interaction matrix identify ways in which learners and Scripture might interact in the context of the Bible study. The statements relate to personal, communal, and societal expressions of faith.

Statements in the Teaching Strategies matrix suggest ways for writers to create sessions that connect Scripture and learners through a variety of educational methods that take into account the different ways people learn.

Statements in the Special Interest Matrix identify ways writers might address topics of special concern that are particularly appropriate to the Scripture text: handicapping conditions, racial and ethnic issues, drug and alcohol abuse, and ecology, for example. While the Faith Interaction matrix provides the beginning point for each session in a book in the *Great Themes of the Bible,* learning goals employed by the writers arise from all these matrices.

Great Themes of the Bible Provides Opportunities for Spiritual Growth

The books in *Great Themes of The Bible* offer you an opportunity to see the vital connection between daily life and the Bible. Every session begins and ends with worship in order to help you experience God's presence as you participate in the sessions. The small group sessions also provide opportunities to develop friendships with others that are based upon respect, trust, and mutual encouragement in faith formation.

WELCOME TO *GREAT THEMES OF THE BIBLE*

The following principles guide our approach to spiritual growth and faith formation:

- Faith and life belong together. We seek to discover connections or crossing points between what God reveals in the Bible and the needs, choices, and celebrations of our ordinary experience. Biblical themes provide this crossing point.
- Everyone is a theologian. *Theology* may be defined as "loving God with our minds" as well as with our hearts. All in your group, regardless of background, are fully qualified to do that.
- Adults learn best through reflection on experience. No longer are we blank tablets on which new knowledge must be imprinted. We can draw on a fund of experience and ask what it means for us in light of Scripture and Christian teaching about God and creation.
- Questions stimulate spiritual growth more than answers. An authoritative answer seems final and discourages further thinking, while a stimulating question invites further creative exploration and dialogue.
- Learning involves change, choice, and pain. If we are to take seriously what God is telling us in Scripture, we must be open to changing our opinions, making new lifestyle choices, and experiencing the pain of letting go of the old and moving into a new and unknown future, following the God of continuing creation.
- Community sharing fosters spiritual growth. When a group commits to struggling together with questions of faith and life, they share personal experiences, challenge assumptions, deepen relationships, and pray. God's Spirit is present. The God of continuing creation is at work.

We pray that you will experience the freedom to ask questions as you explore the great themes in your life and in the Bible. We pray that you will encounter and experience the life-transforming love of God as you become part of a *Great Themes of the Bible* group. And finally, we pray that you will see yourself as a beloved human being created in the image of God and that you will grow in your love of God, self, and neighbor.

Using the Books in *Great Themes of the Bible*

Each book in the *Great Themes of the Bible* series has within its pages all you need to lead or to participate in a group.

At the beginning of each book you will find:

- suggestions for organizing a *Great Themes of the Bible* small group.
- suggestions for different ways to use the book.
- suggestions for leading a group.
- an introduction to the great theme of the Bible that is at the center of all the sessions.

In each of the seven sessions you will find:

- a focus statement that illuminates the particular issues and questions of the theme in contemporary life and in the Scriptures for the session.
- opening and closing worship experiences related to the focus of each session.
- concise, easy-to-use leader/learner helps placed in boxes near the main text to which they refer.
- main content rich with illustrations from contemporary life and reliable information about the Scriptures in each session.

In the Appendix you will find:

- a list of Scriptures that illuminate the biblical theme.
- information about The Committee on the Uniform Series.
- information about other Bible study resources that may interest your group.

Books in the *Great Themes of the Bible* series are designed for versatility of use in a variety of settings.

Small Groups on Sunday Morning. Sunday morning groups usually meet for 45 minutes to an hour. If your group would like to go into greater depth, you can divide the sessions and do the study for longer than seven weeks.

Weekday or Weeknight groups. We recommend 60 to 90 minutes for weekday/weeknight groups. Participants should prepare ahead by reading the content of the session and choosing one activity for deeper reflection and study. A group leader may wish to assign these activities.

A Weekend Retreat. For a weekend retreat, distribute books at least two weeks in advance. Locate and provide additional media resources and reference materials, such as hymnals, Bibles, Bible dictionaries and commentaries, and other books. If possible, have a computer with Internet capabilities on site. Tell participants to read their study books before the retreat. Begin on Friday with an evening meal or refreshments followed by gathering time and worship. Review the introduction to the theme. Do the activities in Session 1. Cover Sessions 2, 3, 4, 5, and 6 on Saturday. Develop a schedule that includes time for breaks, meals, and personal reflection of various topics and Scriptures in the sessions. Cover Session 7 on Sunday. End the retreat with closing worship on Sunday afternoon.

Individual Devotion and Reflection. While the books are designed for small-group study, they can also be beneficial for individual devotion and reflection. Use the book as a personal Bible study resource. Read the Scriptures, then read the main content of the sessions. Adapt the questions in the leader/learner boxes to help you reflect upon the issues related to the biblical theme. Learning with a small group of persons offers certain advantages over studying alone. In a small group, you will encounter people whose life experiences, education, opinions and ideas, personalities, skills, talents, and interests may be different from yours. Such differences can make the experience of Bible study richer and more challenging.

Organizing a *Great Themes of the Bible* Small Group

Great Themes of the Bible is an excellent resource for all people who are looking for meaning in their daily lives, who want to grow in their faith, and who want to read and reflect upon major themes in the Bible. They may be persons who are not part of a faith community yet who are seekers on a profound spiritual journey. They may be new Christians or new members who want to know more about Christian faith. Or they may be people who have been in church a long time but who feel a need for spiritual renewal. All such persons desire to engage more deeply with issues of faith and with the Bible in order to find meaning and hope.

Great Themes of the Bible is an excellent small-group study for those who have completed *Beginnings,* a program that introduces the basics of Christian faith. It is ideal for those who are not yet involved in an ongoing Bible study, such as *Adult Bible Studies,* DISCIPLE, *Genesis to Revelation,* and *Journey Through the Bible,* or for those who prefer short-term rather than long-term studies. *Great Themes of the Bible* also provides a point of entry for those who have never been involved in any kind of Bible study.

Starting a *Great Themes of the Bible* study group is an effective way to involve newcomers in the life of your local church. If you want to start a *Great Themes of the Bible* small group as part of the evangelism program in your local church, follow the steps below:

- Read through the *Great Themes of the Bible* study book. Think about the theme, the issues generated by the theme, and the Scriptures. Prepare to respond to questions that someone may ask about the study.

- Develop a list of potential participants. An ideal size for a small group is 7 to 12 people. Your list should have about twice your target number (14 to 24 people). Have your local church purchase a copy of the study book for each of the persons on your list.

- Decide on a location and time for your *Great Themes of the Bible* group. Of course, the details can be negotiated with those persons who accept the invitation, but you need to sound definitive and clear to prospective group members. "We will initially set Wednesday night from 7 to 9 P.M. at my house for our meeting time" will sound more attractive than "Well, I don't know either when or where we would be meeting, but I hope you will consider joining us."

- Identify someone who is willing to go with you to visit the persons on your list. Make it your goal to become acquainted with each person you visit. Tell them about *Great Themes of the Bible*. Give them a copy of the Great Themes study book for this group. Even if they choose not to attend the small group at this time, they will have an opportunity to study the book on their own. Tell each person the initial meeting time and location and how many weeks the group will meet. Invite them to become part of the group. Thank them for their time.

- Publicize the new *Great Themes of the Bible* study through as many channels as are available. Announce it during worship. Print notices in the church newsletter and bulletin and on the church Web site if you have one. Use free public event notices in community newspapers. Create flyers for mailing and posting in public places.

- A few days before the session begins, give a friendly phone call or send an e-mail to thank all persons you visited for their consideration and interest. Remind them of the time and location of the first meeting.

For more detailed instructions about starting and maintaining a small group, read *How to Start and Sustain a Faith-based Small Group*, by John D. Schroeder (Abingdon, 2003).

Leading a *Great Themes of the Bible* Small Group

A group may have one leader for all the sessions, or leadership may be rotated among the participants. Leaders do not need to be experts in Bible study because the role of the leader is to facilitate discussion rather than to impart information or teach a particular content. Leader and learner use the same book and share the same commitment to read and prepare for the *Great Themes of the Bible* session each week. So what does the leader actually do?

A Leader Prepares for the Session

Pray. Ask for God's guidance as you prepare to lead the session.

Read. Read the session and its Scriptures ahead of time. Jot down questions or insights that occur during the reading. Look at the leader/learner helps in the boxes.

Think about group participants. Who are they? What life issues or questions might they have about the theme? about the Scriptures?

Prepare the learning area. Gather any needed supplies, such as sheets of newsprint, markers, paper and pencils, Bibles, hymnals, audio-visual equipment, masking tape, a Bible dictionary, Bible commentaries, a Bible atlas. If you are meeting in a classroom setting, arrange the chairs in a circle or around a table. Make sure that everyone will have a place to sit.

Prepare a worship center. Find a small table. Cover it with an attractive cloth. Place a candle in a candleholder on the center. Place matches nearby to light the candle. Place a Bible or other items that relate to or illuminate the session focus on the worship center.

Pray. Before the participants arrive, pray for each one. Ask for God's blessing on your session. Offer thanks to God for the opportunity to lead the session.

A Leader Creates a Welcoming Atmosphere

Hospitality is a spiritual discipline. A leader helps to create an environment that makes others feel welcome and that helps every participant experience the freedom to ask questions and to state opinions. Such an atmosphere is based upon mutual respect.

Greet participants as they arrive. Say their names. If the group is meeting for the first time, use nametags.

Listen. As group discussion unfolds, affirm the comments and ideas of participants. Avoid the temptation to dominate conversation or "correct" the ideas of other participants.

Affirm. Thank people for telling about what they think or feel. Acknowledge their contributions to discussion in positive ways, even if you disagree with their ideas.

A Leader Facilitates Discussion

Ask questions. Use the questions suggested in the leader/learner helps or other questions that occurred to you as you prepared for the session. Encourage others to ask questions.

Invite silent participants to contribute ideas. If someone in the group is quiet, you might say something like: "I'm interested in what you are thinking." If they seem hesitant or shy, do not pressure them to speak. Do communicate your interest.

Gently redirect discussion when someone in the group dominates. You can do this in several ways. Remind the group as a whole that everyone's ideas are important. Invite them to respect one another and to allow others the opportunity to express their ideas. You can establish a group covenant that clarifies such respect for one another. Use structured methods such as going around the circle to allow everyone a chance to speak. Only as a last resort, speak to the person who dominates conversation after the group meeting.

Be willing to say, "I don't know." A leader is also a learner. You are not "teaching" a certain content to a group of "students." Instead, you are helping others and yourself to engage the great themes of the Bible as points of crossing to contemporary life and faith formation.

Introducing the Great Theme

CHRIST

Jesus' Life, Teaching, and Ministry

In this volume, the focus is Jesus, who calls us to community and discipleship. Our objective is to try to understand how the uniqueness of his humanity moved his followers to call him "the Christ, the Son of God." Scriptures from Mark will cover Jesus' life from the time of his baptism through his death and resurrection, Scriptures from Matthew will tell about Jesus' ministry of teaching, and Scriptures from Luke will focus on Jesus' ministry of compassion.

A word about titles. The term *messiah* is the English translation of the Hebrew word that means "anointed one." The name *Christ* is the Greek translation of the same term. Therefore, *Christ* as applied to Jesus is a title rather than a name. The early church taught that Jesus was the long-expected Jewish messiah.

A continuing study of the Gospels will take us on a never-ending and life-changing adventure as we become closer and closer to this Jesus Messiah.

The Faces of Jesus is a book that provides a stunning display of artistic images of Jesus in a variety of cultures. Through the media of paintings, sculptures, fabrics and other forms, artists throughout the centuries have envisioned for us the figure of a man they had seen only in their imagination.[1]

As we study these renderings, we see Jesus as Chinese, African, Latino, Irish, and Eskimo. The man from Nazareth who never traveled far from his place of birth is today so universal that he is at home in every land.

The existence of this multitude of images presents us with two levels of understanding of Jesus. The first is that, even though he lived in a particular time and place in a particular culture and historical circumstance, his significance is not thereby limited. He is a presence so universal that each of us can know him—and be known *by* him—on the most intimate terms. Thus we can speak of Jesus as one who is a friend and companion who cares so much for us that he walks with us on our life's journey. Jesus is near.

The other level of understanding that these images suggest is that, as knowable as Jesus is, there is in Jesus that which is beyond our knowing. In Jesus, God became human. Paul speaks of this when he says, "In Christ God was reconciling the world to himself" (2 Corinthians 5:19). Jesus' early followers suggested the divine/human nature of Jesus through such titles as *Son of God, Savior, Lord, Messiah, King of kings* and, most commonly, *the Christ.*

The purpose of this introduction is to let readers know that as we study together Jesus' life, ministry of teaching, and ministry of compassion, we will, at best, open only a window on him. For over 2,000 years there have been countless books written in the study of Jesus; there have been works of art and hymns and musical masterpieces inspired by his life; and there have been a multitude of Christian denominations that claim Jesus as their Lord. So our focus on Jesus will be suggestive rather than exhaustive. For those who are newly acquainted with Jesus, this study will hopefully excite a curiosity to know more of this incredible man. For those for whom Jesus is an old friend, the hope is that our study together will arouse an even greater curiosity about him, lead to a deeper intimacy with him, and inspire a greater awe of what God is doing through him.

Knowledge of Jesus is, first, an inward journey. As we read the Gospel accounts, we may feel admiration, perhaps awe, as we see him heal a blind man, attract a multitude by his preaching, party with social outcasts, and confront religious leaders for their hardness of heart. Yet such admiration is only a beginning of our life with Jesus. Jesus starts to become a life-changing power in our lives when we allow him to heal our spiritual blindness, challenge our self-righteousness, and invite us to work with him among the rejected.

The inwardness of knowing Jesus will surprise us as it stirs up in us an insatiable longing to share what we have received. In Jesus' first sermon in Nazareth, Jesus quoted from Isaiah 61 as the declaration of his calling: "The Spirit of the LORD is upon me, / because he has anointed me to bring good news to the poor. / He has sent me to proclaim release to the captives / and recovery of sight to the blind, / to let the oppressed go free, / to proclaim the year of the Lord's favor" (Luke 4:18-19).

To know Jesus is to encounter God in that same call and to join Jesus in following it.

As you move forward on your journey with Jesus, I encourage you to be patient with yourself. Be assured that Jesus welcomes you as you are into his fellowship. He is eager for you to know the infinite love of God, and this knowledge will grow gradually in God's own time. The journey with Jesus will be exciting and empowering as it was for the first disciples; and through him will flow an infinite stream of love, forgiveness, and understanding as we awkwardly yet persistently follow in the footsteps of this incredible man.

---

[1] From *The Faces of Jesus,* by Frederick Buechner (Harpercollins, 1989).

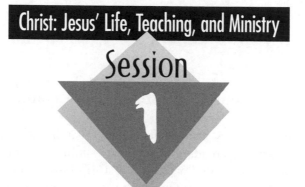

Session

1

POWER TO LEAD

Mark 1:4-13; 2:1-12

This session explores Jesus' baptism, temptation, and miracles and the implications for how God prepares us for leadership.

GATHERING

Enjoy refreshments as you greet one another. Tell about an experience of having to lead. What was it like? What resources did you have? How did you feel about the role? Did you feel adequate? Why or why not?

Sit in a circle for a time of silent prayer. Conclude the silent time with these words from Mark 1:11: "You are my Son, the Beloved; with you I am well pleased." Consider what the words say about God's regard for you. Repeat Mark 1:11 as a closing prayer.

Finding Confidence as a Leader

A first-year seminary student, feeling overwhelmed by the class lectures and the assigned reading, stopped two of his professors in the hall one day. "I am so frustrated with all this stuff I have to learn, I'm about ready to quit. Would someone please tell me in plain, simple words just what is the gospel of Jesus Christ all about?"

The two professors looked at each other, and as if on cue, broke into song:

"Jesus loves me, this I know, for the Bible tells me so . . ."

It is easy to forget that it really is that simple. When Jesus heard the voice of God claiming him as his beloved, that voice was speaking to us as well. Whatever happens, we remain eternally beloved in God's heart. Our name is written on God's heart.

This self-knowledge—that we are always beloved of God—can give us the confidence to lead, to learn from our mistakes and become even stronger leaders. Leadership is a faith issue. When we are challenged about our faith by a skeptic, our confidence in God's love can free us to admit that we do not always have the right answer. Faithful leadership involves allowing ourselves to respond to God's empowerment through the Holy Spirit as we offer ourselves and our gifts to serving God and others.

> *What connections do you make between the assurance that God loves us and our capacity to live as faithful leaders?*

Father Monroni and Helen

Father Monroni was a beloved priest who served a parish in a poor city neighborhood. Helen, a parishioner, was head nurse in a hospital in the community. The limited nursing staff was underpaid and overworked, a source of considerable discouragement to Helen. From time to time she would unburden herself with her pastor.

Fr. Monroni had grown up in poverty. That experience taught him that poverty exists, not because people are lazy, but because the economic system is rigged against the workers and in favor of the owners. There is an imbalance of power.

With this knowledge, Fr. Monroni inspired many people in his parish to take on challenges they might otherwise feel were beyond them. So it was that he encouraged Helen to begin the process of organizing all the nurses so that, together, they could negotiate with the hospital board of directors, thus shifting the balance of power. She followed his suggestions and, with his regular encouragement, Helen led the nurses in forming an organization. Their representatives met with the board to discuss issues relating to their work. Eventually the board agreed to raise salaries and provide health coverage and other new benefits. These changes resulted in better working conditions and improved care for patients.

> *How does Father Monroni display leadership qualities? How does Helen display them? Think of someone whose example or influence has enabled you to bring forth strong qualities you did not realize you had. How did this influence come about? What did you do with your newly discovered strengths? What were some of the outcomes? In what ways have you helped others to discover their strengths?*

Note that Fr. Monroni advised and encouraged Helen; he did not do the work of organizing for her. That is to say, he empowered her. She already possessed the skills and courage needed.

Some Questions About a Baptism

> *Read Mark 1:4-11. What about this Scripture invokes your curiosity? What challenges you? What makes you want to know more? What do you make of Jesus' baptism?*

In Mark's Gospel, Jesus' ministry and leadership began with his baptism. Almost from the outset, Mark confronts us with a dilemma. After announcing that this Gospel is "about Jesus Christ, the Son of God," Mark describes a scene in which this Jesus stands in line with sinners and submits to "a baptism for the forgiveness of sin." We cannot help asking, "What's going on here? Why, of all people, would *Jesus* participate in such a ritual?"

Trying to make sense of this apparently contradictory situation, our immediate explanation might be that Jesus wanted to begin his work by identifying with the people to whom he would be ministering. Yet this interpretation is not fully satisfying. Well, then, how about this: Jesus chose baptism as a kind of ordination vow in which he committed himself fully to God's call. That is, he made a decisive break with his past, separating himself from his family, his career as a carpenter, his life in Nazareth, in order to take on God's calling.

Does this explanation make sense? Yes, but something is still missing. The part about "repentance for the forgiveness of sins" is still hanging there like a giant question mark. If Jesus is the Messiah, how could he have sins of which to repent?

The Beloved Son

Following Jesus' baptism, Mark says, "And just as he was coming up out of the water, he saw the heavens torn apart and the Spirit descending like a dove on him. And a voice came from heaven, 'You are my Son, the Beloved; with you I am well pleased'" (1:10-11).

We should not miss the significance of the timing of this charismatic experience. Jesus heard this voice at the

---

Joseph

Joseph, we hardly knew you,
hewer of wood
faithful husband
loving stepfather.
You taught this child of Bethlehem
a craftsman trade.
Did you also affirm
his holy calling?
Was it you who taught him
to believe in himself
to stand his ground
to trust his vision?
Was it from you he learned
to hold women in high regard
to see the image of God in small
children
to struggle for justice for the
oppressed?
We hardly knew you, Joseph.
Yet we wonder:
Was it because of you he felt so at
home with God as "Abba"?[1]

What are the implications for leadership in this poem? Who have been our models? What did we learn from them? How have we modeled leadership for others? What can we learn about God through the examples of other people?

beginning of his ministry, that is, *before* he had proved his faithfulness. We would not be surprised that he would hear this voice as he hung on the cross, the voice of God's affirmation of him after he had staked his life on God's promise. However, to hear the divine blessing at the beginning of his ministry is so revealing, not only of Jesus' relationship to God, but of ours as well.

We know so little about Jesus' family background that we can only speculate about it. The fact that Jesus' name for God is "Father," and he even called him "Abba," an intimate term equivalent to "daddy," may indicate that Jesus' image of God was profoundly shaped by his relationship to his own father, Joseph. In any case, Jesus, in the life we know about, demonstrated a self-reliance and healthy self-love that must have had its foundation in his profound belief that God's love for him was eternal and unconditional.

Consider how this relationship guided and sustained Jesus throughout his ministry. It gave him confidence to preach boldly, to call followers, to heal the sick, to challenge hypocritical religious critics, to befriend social outcasts, to treat women as equals, and to continue his ministry when confronted with stiff opposition. This relationship with God also undergirded Jesus when he lost his temper, became discouraged about his mission, was tempted to give up and abandon his calling, or had thoughts of using his power for his own selfish purposes.

We should not overlook the implications of our own belovedness in God's eyes. We do not do anything to deserve it. We do not have to earn it. It is a given. That God's love for us is unending and unconditional is the most important fact we shall ever know about God's relationship to us.

Dealing
With Temptation

After Jesus heard the voice from heaven, the story took a surprising turn. In verses 12-13, Mark writes, "And the Spirit immediately drove him out into the wilderness. He was in the wilderness forty days, tempted by Satan; and he was with the wild beasts; and the angels waited on him." (See other versions of this story in Matthew 4:1-11 and Luke 4:1-13.)

The wilderness was a crucial part of Israel's history. After the deliverance from Egyptian slavery, the Israelite people wandered in the wilderness 40 years ("40 years" representing a long time) in search of a homeland. It was a period of great stress, and at times they were not sure they would last. They came close to starving, and at times they grumbled and complained. Yet it was there that they not only survived but also became truly formed as a community, learning in the process how dependent they were on God for their very existence. God provided the miraculous gifts of manna and quail and water, gave them the Law, and guided them to a homeland, a land "flowing with milk and honey."

> *Read Mark 1:9-13. What does "wilderness" symbolize for you? Desolation? isolation? hopelessness? death? A desert can be a place that stores secret life. For example, after a hard rain in the Arizona desert, some hikers were able to identify more than 100 species of flowers that bloomed within days of the rain. How might wilderness experiences in life become the source of unexpected new life? How have we sensed God's presence while going through such experiences? Read Isaiah 35:1.*

So perhaps "wilderness" symbolizes a time of testing, a time of learning that life is sustained entirely by God's grace. It was indeed a time of testing for Jesus. After having heard God's confirming voice and doubtless experiencing the overpowering feeling of God's call, how appropriate that Jesus felt impelled by the Spirit to go on retreat in order to contemplate that call. Jesus must have felt greatly empowered by the call, but empowerment carries with it the potential for doing good and evil. Can you imagine, for example, how coming into a rich inheritance might distort and confuse your judgment? Those who are most likely to be led astray by such wealth are those who have little self-awareness.

The Humanity of Jesus

Thus the Spirit drove Jesus into the wilderness to deal directly with Satan, to wrestle with his dark side. Here, at last, we come to an answer to the question, Why would Jesus Christ, the Son of God, need to submit to "a baptism of repentance for the forgiveness of sins" and to a time of temptation in the wilderness? For those of us who have grown up having heard repeatedly great exaltations of Jesus as Savior, Lord, King of kings, the notion of Jesus' humanity may be difficult. We may put Jesus on a pedestal, isolating him from our daily lives. We have ascribed to him special powers and unique qualities that are denied ordinary mortals such as ourselves. In other words, we have essentially rejected the reality of the Incarnation, God becoming one of us. The story shows us through Jesus what it means to be a child of God, to respond to God's call, and to triumph over temptation.

God's great gift to us in Jesus is precisely Jesus' humanity. That humanity was Jesus' daily reality throughout his life, long before such titles as *Christ, Lord,* and *Savior* were ascribed to him. Read the Gospels and find some of the instances in which Jesus' humanity was revealed.

- Jesus did not carry out his mission alone but counted on others to help him (Mark 1:16-20).
- Jesus and Peter argued about Jesus' mission (Mark 8:27-33).
- Jesus refused to help a woman because she was a foreigner. She then talked him into changing his mind (Mark 7:24-30).
- Jesus became angry with his critics (Mark 3:1-6).
- Jesus was sometimes impatient with the disciples for their lack of faith (Mark 4:35-41; 9:14-29).
- Jesus became exhausted from his work and sought time away for rest (Mark 6:30-31).
- Jesus angrily drove money-changers from the Temple (Mark 11:15-18).
- Jesus agonized over his coming death and begged God to deliver him (Mark 14:32-37).
- On the cross, Jesus expressed doubt about God's being with him (Mark 15:33-34).

> *What images do you have of Jesus? What does savior mean to you? Saved from what? How? What about the idea that Jesus was fully human? What is your reaction to Wink's idea that "the goal of life, then, is not to become something we are not— divine—but to become what we truly are—human"? What are the implications for leadership?*

What becomes abundantly clear in the Gospels is that our humanity is not condemned but affirmed. The miracle revealed in Jesus is not about the divine possibilities of mortals but about the humanity of God, as New Testament scholar Walter Wink points out: "The goal of life, then, is not to become something we are not—divine—but to become what we truly are—human. We are not required to become divine: flawless, perfect, without blemish. We are invited simply to become human, which means growing through our sins and mistakes, learning by trial and error, being redeemed over and over from our compulsive behavior—becoming ourselves, scars and all. It means embracing and transforming those elements in us that we find unacceptable. It means giving up pretending to be good and, instead, becoming real."[2]

A Community Miracle

In Mark's Gospel, Jesus' ministry begins with a series of healing events. Wink's insight about God's gift of our humanity is illustrated in the story of Jesus' healing of the paralytic in Mark 2:1-12. Crucial to the story is the role played by the friends of the sick man. Note how determined they were to get their friend healed and the lengths they went to in bringing him to Jesus. How awkward it must have been to lift the man onto the roof, then open the roof, and let him down into Jesus' presence. This episode had the potential for being a total fiasco and a major embarrassment for the sick man and all his helping friends. What if Jesus could not heal him and the man had to be carried away on his cot? So the risk-taking by the friends was a model of love, faith, and persistence as attributes of leadership in a Christian life.

In our everyday efforts to live out our faith, we may function like the friends of the paralyzed man. We may drive people to doctor's appointments, deliver food to senior citizens, or reach out in other ways to get people the help they need. Christian faith calls us to compassion for others as well as to faith in Christ. Our response to such compassion demonstrates leadership in faith.

Not only does Mark's account illustrate the compassion of Jesus and of the friends, it provides the occasion for Jesus to proclaim the nature of his authority. Illness was believed to be the result of one's sin or the sin of one's parents. To forgive sin was to offer healing. Jesus challenges the accusation of blasphemy with the actual physical healing. "Which is easier, to say to the paralytic, 'Your sins are forgiven,' or to say, 'Stand up and take your mat and walk'? But so that you may know that the Son of Man has authority on earth to forgive sins"—he said to the par-

> *Read Mark 2:1-12. What does this story say to you about Jesus? about the friends? about those who witnessed the healing? How does it illuminate Jesus' ministry? What does it say to you about being a leader?*

alytic—"I say to you, stand up, take your mat and go to your home" (Mark 2:9-11). "Son of Man" could mean either "human being" or a messianic figure associated with a restored Israel. In either case, authority is marked by compassion that overrules conventional wisdom. Jesus offered wholeness to the paralytic through forgiveness and healing. In so doing he pronounced his authority and leadership as Son of Man.

Empowered by God

Mark's story of Jesus' baptism, temptations, and miracles is revealing of how Jesus was empowered by God to embark on a radical, high-risk

CLOSING WORSHIP

Read or sing the hymn "Here I Am, Lord." Pray the following prayer as a closing: "God of all people, help us to know your deep love for us. Help us to discover who we can be by looking at Jesus. Give us his heart and his confidence. In Christ we pray. Amen."

ministry that cost him his life yet eventually changed the world. We are likewise empowered by God to offer to those around us more compassion, wisdom, and inner strength than we ever dreamed was possible.

God's love claims us, thus empowering us to be agents of healing and hope in a world that is hungering for the gospel's good news.

---

[1]"Joseph," by Harry C. Kiely.

[2]From *The Human Being: Jesus and the Enigma of the Son of Man*, by Walter Wink (Augsburg Fortress Publishers, 2001); page 29.

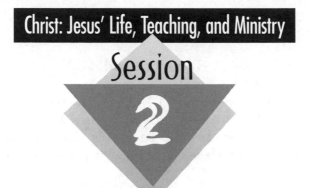

Session

2

THE PREVAILING GOOD

Mark 14:53-65; 15:1-5; and 16:1-8

This session recounts the trials, crucifixion, and resurrection of Jesus and what these events teach us about the costs and rewards of faithfulness.

GATHERING

Prior to the meeting, prepare name tags, printing names of individuals famous for having remained steadfast while enduring bitter opposition (for example, Stephen, Peter, Paul, Joan of Arc, Rosa Parks, and Nelson Mandela). Pin a tag to the back of each participant, without disclosing the name on it, explaining that this person showed great courage while taking a controversial stand. Invite them to play a guessing game of "Who Am I?"

Sit in a circle for a time of silent prayer. Pray these words from the psalmist: "I believe that I shall see the goodness of the LORD / in the land of the living. / Wait for the LORD; / be strong, and let your heart take courage; / wait for the LORD!" (Psalm 27:13-14).

"Here I Stand!"

The place is the City School of Nursing. The year is 1958. All day Friday, at the end of an intense first week, the 19 young women who made up the first-year class had been excited as they talked about going swimming in the school's indoor pool that afternoon. What a perfect break!

Alice was quite animated as she returned to her dormitory room and began to put on her swimsuit. She noticed, however, that Shirley, her roommate, was reclining in an easy chair, reading.

"Hey, Shirley, aren't you going swimming?" asked Alice.

"No, I need to do some studying," Shirley responded.

"Oh, come on. You need a break. You've got all weekend to study."

As Alice continued to appeal to Shirley, the real reason for her decision finally came out. The school did not allow "racial mixing" in the swimming pool. In this mostly all-white class, Shirley was the exception: She was African American.

Alice was outraged. "This is absurd! How can they do such a thing? Well, if you can't join us, then I'm not going either."

"Please don't make a fuss," said Shirley. "I'm okay with this. I'm used to it. Besides, I can use the time to catch up on some studies."

"I will *not* be quiet about this. In fact, I am going to tell the others."

Alice walked up and down the corridor of the dormitory, knocking on doors, informing the other students that the pool was racially segregated. "Shirley won't be allowed to swim with us." Equally incensed, student after student announced their decision not to join in the swim.

"We have to protest this," Alice insisted. So the entire class went to the director of nursing and voiced their complaint. The director was caught off-guard by the protest, but she took time to listen carefully to the students. She was sympathetic to their

> *Think of some situation in which you observed an innocent individual being hurt by an unjust situation. What was the consequence for those involved? Did anyone intervene to set the record straight? How? What happened? What connections do you see between such situations and Christian faith?*

plea but asked them to give her time to discuss the matter with the policy committee.

The faculty was unaccustomed to dealing with organized student protests, so the director's meeting with the policy committee was lengthy and at times contentious. Eventually, however, the issue was resolved in favor of the students' demands. By the following weekend, the segregation policy had been abolished.

The Mass Mind

One secret of Hitler's rule of Germany was the public's gullible acceptance of his declarations that the country's economic recession was the fault of the Jews. A disposition toward anti-Semitism in the public mind made many people vulnerable to Hitler's calculated exploitation. There were, however, some Germans, such as Dietrich Bonhoeffer, who immediately saw through Hitler's demagoguery and who courageously took steps to counter it. The point here is that popular opinion can sweep masses of people along because few individuals take the time and trouble to raise questions. A sign of maturity is one's readiness to think critically about popularly accepted "truths," which may, in fact, be cleverly orchestrated propaganda.

There is abundant evidence that the "mass mind"—where the general population seems to go along unquestioningly with a popular belief—can be dangerous. This phenomenon often manifests itself during a national crisis, for example, during a time of war. If national leaders who make the decision to declare war are determined to squelch dissent, they may invoke patriotism as a device for shaming dissenters into silence. Yet it is precisely in such circumstances that independent opinion is vital to the making

What other persons or situations can you think of in which courageous persons spoke out against injustice and prevailing mass opinion?

of healthy and informed decisions. One of our greatest gifts is the ability to think independently. Thomas Paine, Frederick Douglas, and Susan B. Anthony are examples of individuals who were critical thinkers and courageous leaders who spoke out against prevailing mass opinion. While speaking out may lead to disapproval, or in extreme situations, persecution, we find hope and strength when we stand up for what is right.

Injustice in Jesus' Trial

The anti-Semitism of Hitler's rule and the racism that prohibited Shirley's swimming with her classmates are extreme examples of injustice. Mark's account of Jesus' trial before the Sanhedrin (14:53-65) illustrates another extreme injustice rendered to one who chose to speak out, to heal, and to reveal injustice.

The trial, which ultimately ended in a conviction, was based on trumped up charges. Shirley's exclusion from swimming privileges and the persecution of Jews during the Holocaust were the result of blatant prejudice. The common thread is this: The conviction of Jesus, the exclusion of Shirley, and the persecutions were based on transparent lies. We observe the accusers of Jesus could not even agree on his "crime." It is obvious they were going out of their way to create grounds for executing him. The myth of racial inferiority is the product of prejudice, yet the myth persists because so many people—who should know better—consent to leave the lie unchallenged.

One of Jesus' accusers said, "We heard him say, 'I will destroy this temple that is made with hands, and in three days I will build another, not made with hands'" (Mark 14:58). The accuser was referring to a statement by Jesus to his disciples in response to their admiration of the Temple as such an impressive structure. Jesus' response was, "Do you see these great buildings? Not one stone will be left here upon another; all will be thrown down" (Mark 13: 2). (Note that, counter to their accusation, Jesus did not claim *he* would cause the Temple's destruction.)

> *Read Mark 14:53-65; 15:1-5. Reenact the trial of Jesus based on your reading. What especially strikes you about the trial? What challenges you? How do you interpret Jesus' responses? How does Jesus demonstrate courage?*

The Temple rulers and the thousands of laborers who had erected the structure had a vested interest in its permanence, so they would have been greatly offended at Jesus' lack of reverence for a structure they regarded as holy and eternal. However, Jesus' point was that God could not be contained within any structure made by human hands. Someone has said that "a half truth is like half a brick: You can't build anything with it, but you can throw it a long way." Jesus' enemies, desperate to compile evidence against him, were grasping at half-truths, or rather, at distortions of truth. When the high priest asked Jesus if he was "the Messiah, the Son of the Blessed One," Jesus' response led to the accusation of blasphemy.

Why Did the Authorities Hate Jesus?

Most Christians grew up with a positive image of Jesus. We remember his compassion for the sick, the poor, and the rejected. We remember his parables, the Sermon on the Mount, and his healing of the afflicted. Why would there be such intense hostility toward Jesus, to the point that the religious leaders conspired to have him executed?

> *Why do you think such intense hostility was felt toward Jesus?*

One answer is that Jesus was a non-violent revolutionary who was a threat to the power structure. The Temple authorities had turned the religious rules into self-serving laws that enhanced their power over others. For example, a leper would be excluded from full participation in the life of the community until he had been healed. Only a priest could declare the leper clean (Luke 17:11-19). Jesus' teaching and actions demonstrated that compassion consistently overrules the requirements of religious ritual and practice. He went about healing people, proclaiming such acts as signs of God's reign, and criticizing those in authority who were more concerned with rules than with compassion.

> *Can you think of other religious leaders who were unpopular because they exposed religious frauds? What incidents in contemporary times have created mistrust of religious institutions? What connections do you see between such incidents and the trial of Jesus?*

Another example was the buying and selling that took place in the Temple (Mark 11:15-19). When pilgrims came from distant lands to offer sacrifices in the Temple, they would need to exchange their money for local currency in order to purchase animals for sacrifice. The poor were often charged excessive fees. This is why Jesus chased the moneychangers from the Temple, calling them "robbers" (Mark 11:17).

Jesus had done more than insult the authorities; he had hit at the very nerve of their power and wealth. Many among the Temple rulers were able to get away with extortion by exploiting the religious mystique that held the masses in their sway. Recognizing this perversion of the faith, Jesus, by teaching and example, de-mystified the powers of the religious leaders.

An unfortunate consequence of Jesus' criticism of the religious leaders of the day has been that subsequent generations have often misunderstood the Bible and blamed Jews as a people for the death of Jesus. Such blaming is a terrible abuse of history, of Scripture, and of the teachings of Jesus. Jesus was a Jew. The movement that would become known as Christianity was initially a movement within the Jewish community. Unfairly and inaccurately blaming Jewish people for the death of Jesus has led to prejudice and severe persecution that contradicts everything Jesus taught about the nature of God and the way we should relate to one another.

The Power of Resurrection

As Oscar reached 40, he became increasingly concerned that, if he did not find a significant other soon, he would die a bachelor. He had dated several young women, but none seemed to be "right." That is, except for Eleanor. In so many ways she struck him as a most desirable mate. Several times he had come close to popping the question, but each time he would have second thoughts and would back off. "What's the rush?" he would ask himself. "I'll think about that tomorrow."

What does resurrection mean to you? What contemporary examples from daily life illustrate the power of the Resurrection to you?

So he faced a crisis the day he found that Eleanor, whom he had not seen in weeks, was about to move to a distant city in pursuit of higher education. Suddenly Eleanor seemed like just the right person to be his wife, assuming that she would be agreeable to the idea. However, the thought of making such a serious, lifetime commitment terrified him. "What if she says yes, and then it turns out to be a bad marriage?" he kept asking himself. He paced the floor for hours, weighing the pros and cons of marriage to Eleanor. He prayed for guidance, but no heavenly voice intervened to instruct him.

Finally it dawned on Oscar why he was still a bachelor: fear of commitment. He had kept excusing himself on the grounds that "the right one has not come along." However, now the prospect of losing Eleanor compelled him to do some serious reflection about himself. He was single for one reason—he had been determined to live without risk. When he finally faced up to his faithlessness, he found the courage to propose to Eleanor.

When Oscar and Eleanor celebrated their 20th wedding anniversary with their two children and other family members, Oscar offered a silent prayer of thanksgiving that God had given him the courage to defy the paralyzing fear that had held him back from marriage with all its challenges, heartaches, and fulfillments.

It may be that what underlies all fear is the threat of death. Not necessarily physical death but the prospect of the loss of what we perceive to be life's meaning. Oscar's reluctance to commit to another person was based on the fear that marriage would bring about the loss of certain privileges of bachelorhood (which, of course, it did) and that life in a new context would be a waste. Such fears are not unfounded, for so many marriages end in divorce. Yet only by letting go of an old, fear-ridden life would Oscar be free to enter into the possibilities of a new life. In making the choice to move forward in faith, Oscar was demonstrating the power of the Resurrection. As with the first disciples, new life could begin only by the free abandonment of the old life.

The power of resurrection can be witnessed in other ways in addition to overcoming fear. An alcoholic finds sobriety. In spite of repeated failures, persistence and hard work finally lead to success. In the midst of life-threatening illness, a person finds peace and strength. Resurrection in these illustrations is literally "standing again" and finding new life in any circumstance. Christian faith is a resurrection faith.

Mark's Unique Resurrection Story

Mark's telling of the gospel story seems incomplete. Matthew, Luke, and John describe resurrection appearances by Jesus; but Mark does not. Mark16:9-20, according to many scholars, was not written by Mark but rather was added by a later writer who probably thought Mark's original ending had been lost. As readers, we can identify with the feeling that the abrupt ending (16:1-8) leaves us hanging.

In the story of the women who go to the tomb, Mark says that, in spite of the young man's instructions that they should go to Galilee to meet Jesus, "they went out and fled from the tomb, for terror and amazement had seized them; and they said nothing to anyone, for they were afraid" (16:8).

Read Mark 16:1-8. What challenges you about this ending? What makes you want to know more?

We have traveled this long journey with Jesus and the disciples. We followed Jesus through his trial and crucifixion, and we have read of his promised resurrection. Obviously the omission of that last step is a disappointment. We want to see and hear from the risen Christ!

Yet we know that the story did not end there. The frightened women and the cowardly male disciples who had fled during Jesus' trial experienced an empowering revelation that drove them out into the streets to proclaim Jesus' victory over the grave. As they dared to trust in Jesus' promise—"I will be with you."

What would it mean for us to "go to Galilee" and become a disciple of Jesus? What is a disciple?

New Testament scholar Ched Myers views the ending of this Gospel as having a specific purpose in Mark's telling of the Jesus story.[1] The young man dressed in white reminded the women that Jesus had promised to meet them and the other disciples in Galilee. Why Galilee? Because that is where this Gospel story began. According to Mark, Jesus called his first disciples in Galilee and began his ministry there. If they wanted to see the resurrected Jesus, they would have to go to Galilee. Thus the Jesus story had come full circle.

So what is the message? According to Myers, Mark's Gospel is far more than a story of hope, it is an invitation to discipleship. These followers of Jesus are being told that, with Jesus' resurrection, the story is beginning again. The Resurrection will be revealed to them only as they stake their lives on the gospel, as Jesus did. The old saying "Seeing is believing" is turned on its head. In Mark's telling, *believing* is seeing.

The Resurrection becomes real for us as we trust Jesus' promise through the risk of commitment. We had hoped for a "happy ending"; but the gospel has been proclaimed to us not for our entertainment but to challenge us to take up a new life.

CLOSING WORSHIP

Sing the hymn "He Lives." Pray silently about how you might respond to the power of Jesus' resurrection. How might you express your discipleship?

Close with the following prayer: "O Holy One, who speaks to us out of the empty tomb, open our hearts to the new possibilities that await us. Give us the faith to go to Galilee in the eager expectation that Jesus will meet us there and lead us into a life more rich with hope than we have ever dared to dream. Amen."

---

[1]From *Binding the Strong Man*, by Ched Myers (Orbis Books, 1988); page 399.

Session 3

EXPERIENCING TRUE JOY

Matthew 5:1-16; 6:1-18

This session explores the teachings of Jesus in the collection we call the Sermon on the Mount. They illustrate how living our lives according to the ways of God's realm will lead to true happiness and faithful living.

GATHERING

Prior to the meeting, print out the Beatitudes on letter-size sheets. Print the first half of a beatitude on one sheet and the second half on another. For example: "Blessed are those who mourn" (on one sheet); "for they will be comforted" (on another sheet). Invite participants to take a sheet as they arrive and then locate the person with the other half of the beatitude. When the partners have found each other, tape the completed beatitude to the wall. Discuss whether the pairing in each case is correct and what meaning is expressed in them.

Pray the following prayer: "God of justice, mercy, and love, help us to hear Jesus' teachings about living in your realm. Lead us as we seek ways to discover true happiness by demonstrating justice, mercy, and love everyday. In Christ we pray. Amen.

Happiness

What is happiness? Perhaps happiness brings to mind some of the things that we believe will promote it, such things as financial success, power, fame, honor, or prestige. It might mean living in a beautiful house, wearing fine clothes, or driving a sleek automobile. It could mean health, fitness, and athletic skill.

> *How do you define* happiness? *What do you need in order to be happy?*

Several years ago, a story circulated about a boy who was diagnosed with cancer. His oncologist prescribed a series of chemotherapy treatments. The boy was worried by this bad news, of course; but what bothered him most, it seemed, was when the doctor told him he would lose all his hair until the treatments were finished. Not a happy situation!

Losing his hair would make him look like a freak, he thought; and he dreaded having to go to school and face the other students. "They'll stare at me and make fun of me," he said. "I know they will."

His mother said that she would talk to the teacher and ask her to explain to the other students why Jody was losing his hair.

> *What stories do you know about that demonstrate our capacity to experience joy during times of hardship?*

"No!" he insisted. "I don't want you talking to anybody about it. Besides, I'm not going back to school 'til this is over."

When the teacher told the class about the boy's cancer and the loss of his hair, the disclosure precipitated a creative thought on the part of Jody's best friend. After consulting with his own parents, he showed up at school the next day *completely bald*. The idea caught on, and eventually every boy in the class went to his barber and had his head shaved.

When the boy with cancer returned to class, he stood and stood in the door and looked at the strange sight of a room full of bald-headed boys. Slowly a big smile spread across his face in the presence of a gleeful class. He joined them in having a big laugh.

Happiness, in terms of this world's way of thinking, would mean that the boy would be cured of cancer and would have a full head of hair as he normally would. However, his medical condition prevented that kind of happiness for a time. He and his classmates, however, were in touch with a deeper happiness when they joined him in being bald.

Jesus Teaches About True Happiness

Matthew 5 and 6 contains a collection of teachings traditionally called the "Sermon on the Mount." In these teachings, Jesus points to the true happiness or blessedness that emerges from living according to the ways of God's kingdom or realm. He illuminates relationship with God that leads us to a life of mercy, justice, and love. True happiness emerges from living God's way of life.

The social and political reality that governed the lives of the people during Jesus' life and during the time that Matthew was written was Roman rule. Those who first heard this gospel were an oppressed people, and the teachings speak poignantly to their situation.

Matthew arranges the teachings in a way that evokes the people's awareness of Moses' giving of the Law on the mountain in the wilderness. These teachings of Jesus point to the heart of God's law and teach what it meant—and means—to live in God's realm. These teachings do not replace the Law. They illuminate the Law.

The Beatitudes (Matthew 5:1-16)

As we study the Beatitudes, it is important to remember that Jesus directed these to a community of people who were trying to be faithful followers. New Testament scholar M. Eugene Boring states, "Matthew's beatitudes are not practical advice for successful living, but prophetic declarations made on the conviction of the coming-and-already present kingdom of God."[1] The story of the boy with cancer and the loving support given by his third-grade class can be interpreted as a "sign" of the presence of God's kingdom in everyday life. Through the Beatitudes, Jesus was calling attention to and blessing those God-inspired acts that occur in community. A beatitude that could appropriately be applied to the classroom incident is "Blessed are the merciful, for they will receive mercy" (Matthew 5:7).

The word *blessed* is a translation of the Greek word "makarios," which implies a gift of God and includes "happy" among its meanings.

Read Matthew 5:1-16. How do these blessings differ from our common understanding of happiness? How do they challenge you as you think about contemporary Christian life?

What signs of God's presence and glory can you identify in your life at home or work or your neighborhood? How are they "salt" and "light" to you? How do these signs offer you hope?

What examples or stories do you know about in which the needs of others were taken into account as much as or more than personal need? How do such examples affect your view of humankind?

According to Boring, the Beatitudes are a reversal of the traditional values of society. In place of ordinary life pursuits such as wealth, beauty, and power, the Beatitudes pronounce God's blessing on those who, in their lives of faith, endure poverty, suffer great loss, are persecuted, devote their lives to working for peace and justice. Boring also sees the Beatitudes as more than a command to strive for blessedness. They proclaim the condition of blessedness that already exists, and they contain the implied expectation that members of the community will live in terms of the declared blessedness.[2]

The metaphors of salt and light in Matthew 5:13-16 aptly demonstrate the result of being a faithful disciple. Living according to God's ways of justice, mercy, and love show the "taste" and the "light" of God's glory and presence in our world.

Dr. Pedro Jose Greer Jr. is a Cuban-American doctor who has worked among the poor in Miami for 20 years. He has incredible stories to tell about the generosity of the poor. On one occasion, he met a six-year-old boy who had come to Greer's clinic. Noting that the boy was hungry, Greer gave him a sandwich. The boy took two bites then wrapped the sandwich and put it away. The doctor asked the boy why he did not finish the sandwich. The boy told him he had brothers and they were hungry, too. "People like that little boy are the reason I never run out of hope," said Greer.[3]

Jesus would have cheered the little boy's quiet generosity. It is clear that the boy's sharing was motivated by a concern for his brother rather than a desire for self-promotion. He is a model for us in the church where we often are not only stingy in our giving but also may expect special recognition when we are a little more generous than usual. Jesus' emphasis is on our relationship to God, which is reward enough.

> *Read Matthew 6:1-7. What challenges you about these teachings? How do they speak to practices in contemporary culture? What examples can you think of that illustrate the practice of personal piety as Jesus describes them?*

Honest Piety

Facing the challenges of living daily as committed disciples of Jesus is possible only as our inner lives are developed. Such development often involves the practice of spiritual disciplines. The inner life consists of more than simple practice and rational reflection, however, as important as they are. It also involves our being open to the quiet work of the Spirit. Matthew has assisted us by compiling many of Jesus' teachings about honest piety regarding the spiritual disciplines of almsgiving, prayer, and fasting.

A Quiet Witness

One woman's quiet witness emerged from her discovery of her own deeply ingrained racial prejudice. When Harriet attended the first session of a Lenten morning study group, she found herself seated next to Sarah, an accident that proved to be providential. Harriet was a distinguished, elderly white woman; and Sarah was an equally distinguished and respected African American woman. The study session concluded with a seated communion service, with the bread and the chalice being passed from person to person around the circle.

Following the final "Amen," Harriet abruptly excused herself and quickly made her way to the restroom where she vomited the elements she had just consumed. Having grown up in a community that taught and practiced racial segregation, Harriet had very few encounters with racial minorities as social equals; and drinking after Sarah from the same chalice was an experience that went against all she had learned in her racist upbringing. It literally made her sick to her stomach.

43

How can Harriet's quiet witness inform your own efforts at honest piety? When have you recognized something within your own attitudes that you felt you needed to change? How was God present with you?

Harriet treated her unpleasant experience as a call from God. She had never thought of herself as racist. She was a genteel southern woman who treated all persons respectfully, regardless of their race; but her stomach's revulsion at having drunk from the same cup as Sarah was a wake-up call. She had been deceiving herself about her prejudice, as many of us do. Perhaps out of embarrassment, Harriet was careful not to tell anyone what she was experiencing. Instead, she made it a matter of private prayer. She continued attending the Lenten class and made sure that she sat beside Sarah every week. A very personal spiritual discipline became a quiet public witness.

Prayer: Public and Private

One of the subtle dangers of religious disciplines involves our motivation for the discipline. Jesus' teachings about such practices is that they are not about being "religious" but about affirming our kinship to God and empowering our acts of mercy, justice, and love.

Read Matthew 6. What are your thoughts about the idea of offering prayers at public occasions such as school athletic events and graduation exercises? What would be the purpose of including these prayers? Do you think Jesus meant that we are never to pray in public? Why or why not?

Genuine personal piety does not call attention to itself because its intent is to be open to a personal relationship with God. All too often, we want others to know that we are "good," that we are churchgoers who do the right things. We want others to see and to recognize our generosity and our piety. The motivation involves our own need rather than our relationship with God and with other people. Prayer, public and private, nurtures our capacity to be open to God and to live God's way.

From time to time, a news story appears that tells about a controversy in some community regarding prayer in public schools or at an athletic event. Laws regarding separation of church and state have been invoked in some cases to forbid such prayers. These restrictions often arouse outrage among citizens who regard these laws as attempts to exclude God

> *What does the Lord's Prayer say to you about God? about your life as a Christian?*

from public gatherings. We might ask whether the following words of Jesus are pertinent to this controversy: "Whenever you pray, go into your room and shut the door and pray to your Father who is in secret" (Matthew 6:6).

A Model Prayer

According to the Gospel writers, when the disciples asked Jesus to teach them to pray, he gave them what we have come to call the Lord's Prayer (Matthew 6:9-13). Note the following characteristics of this best known of all Christian prayers:

- God who is omnipotent is immediately addressed in the most intimate terms as a heavenly parent: "Our Father in heaven." This is not only a guide for our own praying but also an insight into Jesus' close relationship to God.
- Coupled with this intimacy is an exaltation of God: "Hallowed be your name."
- The first petition is for the coming of God's complete reign in this world: "Your kingdom come."
- True prayer accepts in advance the will of God and confidently anticipates that the divine plan will be accomplished in this world: "Your will be done, on earth as in heaven."
- As children of God, it is appropriate that we petition God for our physical needs: "Give us this day our daily bread."
- Receiving forgiveness from God is inextricably tied to our forgiving others: "And forgive us our debts, as we have forgiven our debtors."
- We pray that God will give us the strength to resist temptation: "And do not bring us to the time of trial, but rescue us from the evil one."[4]

A Church Changes

The teachings of Jesus in Matthew 5 and 6 hold the potential to lead individuals and communities to transformation. Jesus teaches that blessedness or happiness comes to those who "hunger and thirst for righteousness." The Greek word is *dikaiosune*, which suggests equity, justice, and virtue. A pastor told me about an incident in which one of the churches that he served was transformed when they chose to seek righteousness in a concrete way.

Read Matthew 5:6. How is righteousness shown in the story of refurbishing the house for a family? What does it mean to "hunger and thirst for righteousness"? How are we filled through such longing for righteousness? In what ways does your congregation hunger and thirst for righteousness? What might your congregation do to express this in ministry to others?

The church was growing fast and needed more parking space. The trustees learned that a recently deceased parishioner owned a house adjacent to church property and that the house was for sale. They acted quickly to purchase the vacant house, intending to tear it down and pave the area for parking.

However, before moving ahead on dismantling the house, the church went through a process of reviewing several options for property use. In the course of this review, a representative from the local Interfaith Housing Coalition was invited to speak to the planning committee about the area's desperate need for housing for homeless families. Several church members present were moved by the stories of persons who lack decent housing. How can we tear down a house, they asked, when there are people who have nowhere to live?

The church members began to plan how the old house could be refurbished and made available for a family that did not have a place to live. As people met to discuss the issue, those who had initially been opposed began to come around. An older church member who had resisted the housing idea later confessed through tears how he did not realize how terribly painful it is to be homeless.

When a family was finally selected, a small group from the church gathered to welcome them. The family, grateful to once again have a home, were pleasantly surprised to find the pantry and the refrigerator stocked with food.

Life in the Spirit

Finding the blessedness that Jesus promises in our daily experiences is possible only as our inner lives grow through daily experiences. The rich inner life that the Beatitudes promise is not just about finding happiness but about being surprised by joy in circumstances that are often very painful. This life in the Spirit also involves our being open to the Spirit's work within us and within our faith community.

Jesus assists us in our quest for God's way of life through teachings that illuminate the characteristics of life in God's realm. The more we prayerfully ponder these remarkable teachings, the more we will be led into the Spirit's depths and empowered to live as Christ teaches us to live. On that quest, we may, at times, become discouraged with ourselves. Those are the times we need Jesus' words of reassurance: "Your Father who sees in secret will reward you" (Matthew 6:6).

CLOSING WORSHIP

Sit quietly for a moment of silent prayer. Prayerfully consider the following questions: What are your personal struggles in deepening your spiritual life? Reflect on a time when the Spirit surprised you and embraced you and reaffirmed God's abundant love for you. How did your life in the fellowship of other Christians contribute to this experience?

Close the session by praying the Lord's Prayer.

---

[1] From *The New Interpreter's Bible* (Abingdon Press, 1995); page 177.

[2] From *The New Interpreters Bible*; page 177.

[3] "Health Care Should Not Be About Money," by Wayne Coffey in *Parade*, September 21, 2003.

[4] From *Oxford NIV Scofield Study Bible* (Oxford University Press, 1984); and *Matthew, Interpretation, A Bible Commentary for Teaching and Preaching*, by Douglas R. A. Hare (John Knox Press, 1993).

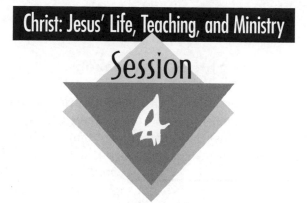

Session

4

JESUS AS STORYTELLER

Matthew 13:1-23; 18:21-35

Everyday life offers many opportunities to learn about living God's kingdom way of life. This session shows how Jesus' use of parables can help us to understand and to practice God's ways in our daily lives.

GATHERING

Write the following Scripture passages from Matthew on small pieces of paper, two pieces of paper for each Scripture: the lamp, 5:15; the weeds, 13:24-30; the mustard seed, 13:31-32; the leaven, 13:33; the treasure hidden in the field, 13:44; the pearl of great price, 13:45-46; the net, 13:47-50; the householder, 13:51-52. Invite each participant to take one piece of paper and then find another person with the same parable on his or her piece of paper. Read and discuss the parables.

Pray the following prayer: "Thank you, O God, for Jesus, who taught us how to look for signs of your Kingdom in the ordinary things of life: mustard seeds, leaven, pearls, fishing nets, even weeds! We pray for an openness of spirit in ourselves that we may recognize these common things as signs of the presence of your Kingdom. Amen."

Stories That Teach

In addition to being a gifted cartoonist, Charles Schultz, author of the comic strip *Peanuts*, was also a committed Christian. It was not unusual that some of his comic strips would build on biblical themes.

One such strip showed Charlie Brown, a principal character in *Peanuts*, on the beach constructing an elaborate sandcastle. He labored at it for some time until his structure was complete. Suddenly a big wave came along and destroyed his handiwork. Charlie Brown, beholding the wreckage with some bewilderment, said, "There's a moral in this somewhere."[1]

> *Read Matthew 7:24-27. What do you see as the moral in the Schultz cartoon and how that relates to Jesus' teaching? What situations in your life might illustrate Jesus' teaching in this parable?*

A person familiar with Jesus' parable about the danger of building a house on sand (Matthew 7:24-27) would likely recognize Schultz's allusion. The ordinary events of life may have a funny side, Schultz might say; but they can also be instructive. Jesus was a teacher who could lead his hearers to profound depths, yet his teaching methods were quite simple so that anyone who had ears to hear would be able to understand their meaning (Matthew 13:9).

A principal characteristic of the gospel Jesus proclaimed was its sheer simplicity, which may help account for the mass of followers. The parables—stories about ordinary things and common experiences—were the heart of his teaching. Hearers could resonate with tales about a poor woman who lost and then found a precious coin, a farmer who unearthed a buried treasure while plowing, a field growing wheat and weeds together, the power of leaven in the loaf, the hated Samaritan who stopped to render aid, the runaway boy who returns

> *What are some parables that open up and enhance your life? What do you hear God saying to you through these simple stories? Make up a parable based on your own experience.*

home. One does not have to have a formal education to be able to partake of the richness of Jesus' parables.

Yet the parables challenge our willingness to hear its deeper message. These stories are not offered to us for entertainment but rather as guideposts for the life of faith. We will know that we have heard the good news when we have listened to a parable so deeply that a voice within us says, "That parable is about me."

The Parable of the Sower

Two wrens found a house suitable to their liking; and after the male had prepared the nest, his partner moved in. Within a few weeks, two fledglings ventured forth, taking flight as the equivalent of mature teenagers who sought their own place in the world. As if this short-term productivity were not enough, the mama and papa wrens soon were making repeated returns to the nest, bringing worms and bugs to feed yet a second brood. When these youngsters were mature enough to take their leave, the parents began to make way for yet a third set of hatchlings.

Read aloud Matthew 13:3-9. What do the images in Jesus' story suggest to you? How does the word listen at the beginning and at the end of the parable strike you? What does it suggest about Jesus' teaching and our response?

All this fecundity is nature's device for assuring the survival of the species. Many of these tiny creatures, as they made their way over thousands of miles of migration, would perish along the journey. Yet enough would survive to assure future generations of wrens.

The principle of nature's abundance underlies Jesus' parable about the farmer's seed-sowing. The seed would fall on many types of soil and only a few of the seeds would actually take root and eventually produce food. Yet the sowing was generous enough that a crop would be assured.

Jesus used this agricultural metaphor to communicate a spiritual reality about life in God's kingdom. In Matthew's Gospel, the parable is followed by an explanation of the use of parables. The disciples asked Jesus, "Why do you speak to them in parables?" Jesus answered,

"To you it has been given to know the secrets of the kingdom, but to them it has not been given."

Further, Jesus explains the parable. What is being sown is the Word, exemplified in his preaching to a variety of audiences. The seed itself is not in question—it is all good seed. What is in doubt is the quality of soil into which each seed falls. These various soils represent the many human responses to the Word.

The sower, according to one interpretation, is God and the seed is Jesus. Furthermore, says Joachim Jeremias, as much as Jesus became the gospel seed, generously sharing himself throughout Judea, his whole ministry was fraught with failure: few converts, much hostility, more and more desertions. As with the farmer's many wasted seeds, much of Jesus' ministry seems to have fallen on unproductive ground. Yet where his seeds did take root in good soil, the harvest was bountiful beyond measure.[2]

Sowing Seeds in Contemporary Life

Marcus lived in a poor community; and he ran with a gang that often got into trouble with the police, mostly for stealing and smuggling drugs. Marcus had been arrested so many times that the neighborhood police recognized him on sight, but then something happened.

What seeds do you see in Marcus's story? What kinds of soil? How does the story offer hope? What connections do you make between the story and the growth of God's kingdom?

The high school football coach saw Marcus playing pass-and-tag one day and was impressed by his running speed and his ability to throw the ball. He took the boy aside and persuaded him to try out for the school team. At first Marcus resisted the discipline required of the boys on the squad, but eventually he got turned around. What made the difference was the coach, who took a personal interest in the boy, challenged Marcus to grow up; and he showed Marcus how to excel in sports. Eventually, the coach became Marcus's father figure, replacing the real father who had abandoned the family when Marcus was a baby.

Feeling that the coach had given him a new lease on life, Marcus imitated the coach by taking a special interest in some of his buddies who were stuck in an old and destructive way of life. On one occasion, he was present at a neighborhood church's teen game lounge when two police officers came in looking for a particular boy who had broken a law and had fled. They spotted the boy, took him into custody, and proceeded to escort him from the building. Teen gangs' hostility toward the police was ongoing anyway, and the sight of one of their own being arrested almost caused a riot.

Outside, the police were wrestling the boy to the ground; but he was quite large and putting up considerable resistance. Marcus, having gone through similar experiences, immediately recognized how dangerous this situation was, so he knelt down beside the boy and begged him not to resist but to cooperate with the police. "You're just making it harder for yourself," pleaded Marcus. Meanwhile, some 40 youth had poured out of the church, raging. They surrounded the police and the boy on the ground. Backup police had not yet arrived.

Some instinct made Marcus take action. Suddenly, he jumped up and yelled, ran through the crowd, and headed down the street. The crowd of youth, with no understanding of what Marcus was doing, instinctively began yelling also and followed him down the street. He continued to run for several blocks as the youth followed. Eventually, the crowd lost interest in the chase and dispersed. Meanwhile, the police handcuffed the youth, who, by now, had stopped resisting, and cooperatively entered the police car. That night, Marcus, through his courage and quick thinking, may have spared someone serious injury, perhaps someone's life.

Thinking back to the parable, we might say that the coach sowed a seed and that, in Marcus's case, it fell on fertile soil. Jesus continues to remind us that "the kingdom of God is at hand," which means that God is forever present in our daily lives finding various ways to sow the seed of ever-new possibilities.

Why Parables?

Why does Jesus rely so heavily on the use of parables in his teaching and preaching? The following passages in Matthew demonstrate some of Jesus' answers when the disciples ask this question:

- Understanding a parable involves a commitment to listen to God's speaking through it. We learn only what we *choose* to learn, and discerning the meaning of the parables means submitting to God's sovereignty (Matthew 13:11).
- Good students—that is, those who truly want to learn—are rewarded for their efforts to try to understand, while those who do not want to learn cheat themselves out of the seed's potentially rich harvest (13:12).
- The disciples, as they partake of the transforming power of the parables, are experiencing a privilege that earlier prophets had longed for but had not heard or seen (13:16-17).[3]

The Challenge of Forgiveness

One of the most challenging aspects of Christian life is the call to forgive and to be forgiven. How do we forgive those who have wronged us? How do we forgive injustice? Is forgiveness a feeling or a choice? Does forgiveness mean that we must tolerate abuse? How do we accept the forgiveness of others or of God? We tangle with such questions every time we encounter a parable that illuminates and illustrates forgiveness.

Jesus' best-remembered parable is the one we call "The Prodigal Son," one of the most moving stories of love and forgiveness in all literature. He called his hearers to forgive others as God had forgiven them. His teaching and preaching about forgiveness is backed up by a life in which he practiced what he beckoned others to do. He gathered his closest friends around him for a last meal, knowing all of them would either betray or abandon him when he most needed them. From the cross, in his dying moments, Jesus prayed for the enemies whose treachery had sealed his fate, saying, "Father, forgive them, for they do not know what they are doing" (Luke 23:34). He taught us to pray, "Forgive us our trespasses as we forgive those who trespass against us," underscoring the reality that it is spiritually impossible to truly accept forgiveness without forgiving others.

What questions do you have about forgiveness? What about the call to forgive or to be forgiven challenges you most?

Seventy Times Seven?

Peter asked a question about forgiveness. "Lord, if another ... sins against me, how often should I forgive? As many as seven times?" Jesus' response greatly increased the number of times to forgive: "Not seven times, but, I tell you, seventy-seven times" (Matthew 18:22). The King James Version says, "seventy times seven." Jesus uses exaggeration to illustrate that forgiveness is not about counting. In fact, it is beyond calculation. A Kingdom parable follows the interaction with Peter, and the parable features forgiveness as an aspect of life in God's realm.

At the heart of Jesus' teaching about forgiveness is that forgiveness received must be forgiveness passed on. The parable of the unforgiving servant (Matthew 18:23-35) underscores this point. The teaching echoes Matthew's version of the Lord's Prayer: "And forgive us our debts, as we also have forgiven our debtors" (Matthew 6:12).

> *Read Matthew 18:21-35. What challenges you about this parable? How does it speak to you about living God's way of life?*

In the parable of the unforgiving servant, we can identify the following important realities about forgiveness:

- Our debt to God (here represented by the king) is so vast there is no way that we could ever—in several lifetimes—pay it back.
- We are totally dependent on God's mercy. That mercy has been extended to us time and time again.
- The debt owed to us by others is miniscule compared to our debt to God.
- We are tempted to exploit the hurt we suffer from others as a source of power over them.
- God's forgiveness is not cheap or easy, as the cross demonstrates. Our willingness to forgive others demonstrates our awareness of God's grace.
- If we withhold forgiveness from those who have hurt us, we keep ourselves from experiencing God's forgiveness.
- No matter how faithful and virtuous a life we lead, we all are perpetually in need of God's grace and mercy.

• When we are merciful toward others, we reflect our deep kinship with God.

Life in God's Kingdom

How does the parable of the unforgiving servant touch on your own personal experiences? Why is forgiving others so hard? When we have been deeply hurt by someone, how do we find the resources for forgiving that person? What happens to us when we nurse a grudge for a long time? How can God help us to let go of the grudge? What do we gain when we are at last free of the grudge?

Jesus' teaching about the kingdom of God often took shape in his parables. His Kingdom teachings essentially illustrate a way of life in which the primary marks are love of God and neighbor. Living this Kingdom way of life also reveals God's presence. Jesus' parables contain the high calling to live and practice the mercy, justice, and love that is God's nature. The parable of the sower and the parable of the unforgiving servant illuminate God's way of life. We are the soil for God's way of life. Our mercy toward others reflects God's mercy.

CLOSING WORSHIP

Sing the hymn "Open My Eyes That I May See."

Close with the following prayer: "What an abundant life you give us, God! You make your presence known in our sisters and brothers and in all the things of your creation, reminders that you are ever near. Thank you for teaching us how to forgive one another by sending your son Jesus to live as one of us, embracing us in his arms of grace. Rekindle our faith so that we depart from this place renewed and recommitted to witnessing to the love of Christ with every person we encounter this week. We pray in Jesus' name. Amen."

SESSION 4: JESUS AS STORYTELLER

[1] From *The Gospel According to Peanuts*, by Robert L. Short (John Knox Press, 1964); pages 27-28.

[2] From *The Parables of the Kingdom*, by Robert Farrar Capon (Eerdmans, 1985); page 69.

[3] From *Rediscovering the Parables*, by Joachim Jeremias (Scribners, 1966); page 120.

[4] From "The Gospel of Matthew," *The New Interpreter's Bible* (Abingdon Press, 1995); pages 303-05.

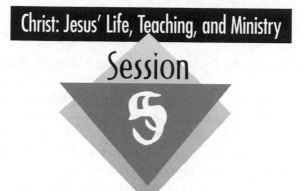

Session

5

LIVING OUR FAITH

Matthew 25:31-46

This session explores how our lives are judged by our deeds of love and mercy.

GATHERING

Find a partner and tell about people you know who give freely of themselves in order to meet the needs of others. Then read aloud Matthew 25:31-46.

Pray the prayer of St. Francis:

> Lord, make us instruments of your peace.
> Where there is hatred, let us sow love;
> where there is injury, pardon;
> where there is discord, union;
> where there is doubt, faith;
> where there is despair, hope;
> where there is darkness, light;
> where there is sadness, joy;
> for your mercy and for your truth's sake. Amen.

Ordinary People and Extraordinary Need

Natalie and Malcolm Kellogg were faced with a very painful task. Because their three-year-old son, Joshua, suffered from severe mental disabilities, they had decided to place him in an institution where he could receive appropriate care—care they had come to realize they simply could not provide. Their decision to take this step had been encouraged by several doctors who had been working with Joshua. The Kelloggs departed early that fateful morning, taking Joshua to court where the legal process for his placement would be fulfilled and Joshua would be taken to his new home.

When Natalie and Malcolm returned home about noon, they found by their front door a pot containing soup and a pan of freshly baked rolls. Amy Stanberry, a new friend who lived nearby, had left these gifts there. Later, as the Kelloggs ate the delicious soup and rolls, they shared their sorrow at having to give up Joshua and their gratitude for Amy's food that nourished their souls and their bodies.

What is particularly challenging about the situation for the Kelloggs? What worries might they have about responses to their decision? How did the Stanberrys' offer of food and friendship meet their need? With whom do you most identify in this story? Why? Are you familiar with other situations like this? Describe one.

The Kelloggs became close friends of Amy and Jack Stanberry; and over time, they discovered that the Stanberrys frequently reached out to care for others. For two years they had provided space in their home for a student from India who had a scholarship but could not afford housing or food. When the Stanberrys, who are white, found that an African American family had been denied a home in their neighborhood, they organized a protest and successfully broke the color barrier. They occasionally planned potluck dinners in their home, inviting every family in the neighborhood. The Stanberrys' lives were filled with examples of caring.

Weapons of the Spirit is the name of a documentary film that tells a remarkable story of courage and compassion during World War II. The year was 1943, during the Nazi reign of terror in Europe. Some 5,000 Jews were transported by rail into the French village of Le Chambon, where they were welcomed and taken into the homes of the residents. The community of 5,000 French Christians provided a safe haven for their guests for four years.

The film was made by Pierre Sauvage who was born on a farm in Le Chambon where his parents were being provided protection. Before coming to Le Chambon, one-third of the Sauvage extended family had been killed in the Nazi concentration camps, so the rescue of 5,000 Jews through the generosity of the Le Chambonaise was a miracle. Pierre Sauvage grew up knowing about this story. As an adult, he decided to return to Le Chambon to see the village and to speak with the few surviving residents who had saved the lives of his family.

> *What contemporary stories do you know about in which ordinary people do extraordinary things to help someone in need?*

Sauvage was told how, on several occasions, the Nazis had sent officials into the village to see if any Jews were being harbored there. The residents of the village kept the Jews in hiding so effectively that the officials were satisfied that no Jews were present. When the victory over Germany was finally announced, all the Jewish residents of Le Chambon immediately packed their bags and returned to their homes. On his visit to Le Chambon, Sauvage asked some of the residents who had been present during the war, "Was it dangerous for you?" "Not at first," one man replied, "but later it was." "Then why did you keep them?" asked Sauvage. One elderly woman, as if the question were a foolish one, answered, "Oh, because we were used to it." What Sauvage found so extraordinary was that the Le Chambonnaise acted as if their heroic behavior had been in no way heroic but was just what any person would do for another in such circumstances.[1]

The massive social problems of our time—hunger, AIDS, terrorism, environmental disasters—seem so daunting that many of us feel helpless to make any difference. Urgent as these issues are, we should not allow them to distract us from the ordinary needs of people we encounter daily—needs to which we *are* able to respond, just as the Stanberrys responded to the Kelloggs.

Persons who have been discriminated against in the place where we work need someone to stand up for and with them. A new immigrant family may need someone to help them navigate the system for becoming naturalized. The local soup kitchen needs more volunteers. A nursing home resident seldom has visitors. Death row inmates are mostly forgotten; names and addresses may be obtained for those willing to correspond. One of our challenges in our needy world is to alert ourselves to the pains and struggles that many people around us go through daily. Our desire to serve Christ will cause us to be alert to the needs of the people we encounter daily. When we pitch in and lend a hand, it helps that person; but it also enriches us in the process. We discover anew the joy of reaching out to others.

A Final Accounting (Matthew 25:31-46)

In Matthew's story of the last judgment, as it has been called traditionally, the reader will look in vain for any mention of doctrinal belief as a requirement for being among those who will "inherit the kingdom." According to this story, we are judged by what we do, or fail to do, to care for our fellow human beings. Consistently, Jesus has described God's will in the Law as self-giving care for others. The way of life in God's kingdom involves the practice of mercy, justice, and love. In the final accounting given by the Son of Man, it is this criteria that determines whether one will live in God's kingdom. Life in God's kingdom consists of service to others.

> *Do a group reading of Matthew 25:31-46 using four "characters" or voices: narrator, the Son of Man, sheep, and goats. What is Jesus getting at? Where do you see yourself in the story? Can you think of times you have been one of the sheep? One of the goats? How is it possible that we could not know when we have or have not ministered to "one of the least of these"? What do you consider to be one of the payoffs for living like the sheep?*

In Matthew's story, the Son of Man identifies with the hungry, the thirsty, the naked, the sick, and the imprisoned. The acts of mercy and justice that we practice toward other human beings demonstrate our love for God. In doing so, however, we are not self-consciously accumulating brownie points with God. Our acts are the fruit of our relationship with God. In similar fashion, the Le Chambonnaise, who seemed totally unimpressed with their own goodness, were living out the call to love their neighbors as if that were a perfectly ordinary thing to do. Theologian Robert McAfee Brown says it well: "The 'righteous' do not claim to be righteous."[2]

Being Held Accountable

The latter part of the story is about those who are condemned because they failed to care for suffering people. The rejection of them is quite severe: "And these will go away into eternal punishment" (25:46). Many people question whether Jesus actually said that because it is so inconsistent with his other teachings and actions. For example, he told Peter to forgive "seventy-seven times" (18:22). Elsewhere Jesus said, "Love your enemies and pray for those who persecute you" (5:44). At the Last Supper, Jesus fed the disciples bread and wine, symbols of his body and blood, even though he knew they would betray or abandon him (26:17-30).

New Testament scholar Walter Wink comments that there is a vindictive streak in Matthew that shows up in several places. We must understand that each of the Gospel writers put together a gospel based on collected stories plus their own understanding of Jesus and his ministry. This means that the personal biases of the writers became part of their Gospels. Apparently Matthew strained under the hostility that his Christian community experienced, and his desire for revenge is reflected in several passages. Thus, in the present passage, because of his certainty that his persecutors will be eternally punished, Matthew puts that judgment in Jesus' mouth.[3] Jesus was capable of anger, but he was not a vindictive person.

Can you cite personal experiences of having been indifferent to the suffering of others? What happened to make you aware? What did you do in response to your awakening? How do you view Christ in the light of your experience?

Simple Justice

Brown says that third-world Christians see in Jesus' story something beyond individual acts of mercy. While Scripture uses the words *righteous* and *unrighteous*, third-world Christians might translate those words as "just" and "unjust," thereby calling attention to the social implications of the story. The Greek word translated "righteous" in verse 46 is *dikaios*, which includes "equitable" and "just" in its meaning. Brown goes further and cites the teaching of the Roman Catholic priest Jose Miranda, who "reminds us that one important aspect of justice involves the restoration of what has been stolen. Giving food to the hungry or clothing to the naked is not a charitable handout but an exercise in simple justice—restoring to the poor what is rightfully theirs, what has been taken from them unjustly."[4]

If Matthew's story is a call to minister to oppressed individuals, it is also a call to apply it on a broad social scale. The church has sometime been found supporting social injustice. In the days of slavery, for example, there were churches, including Methodist, that supported such a reprehensible practice. Later, the civil rights movement exposed the reality that there were many white churches that opposed the civil rights movement and even refused to allow African Americans to attend their services of worship.

Whether the issue is racial integration, peace with justice, promoting a living wage, or other social justice issues, the church has often avoided taking unpopular stands for fear of losing members and financial support. Yet there are also examples of churches living up to the call for social justice, as with Martin Luther King Jr. and the civil rights movement, and former Catholic priest Philip Berrigan, who spent a total of 11 years in prison for his vigorous but non-violent protests against nuclear armament.

One reason the church has sought safety on the sideline of social justice is that many Christians believe that the gospel of Jesus Christ applies only to personal matters. This point of view has led us to support soup kitchens and homeless shelters (which, of course, we should) but to do so as an alternative to correcting the social practices that *result* in poverty.

Ours is the wealthiest nation in history, yet there are millions of people who work at minimum wage, some holding down two or three jobs, who do not have decent housing or health-care insurance or nourishing meals. These are systemic problems, problems that exist because the economic system is defective. If the church joins the struggle for universal health care, a national living wage, and affordable housing, we will doubtless encounter resistance and controversy, just as Jesus did. Yet as we take on such a ministry, we will hear a distant voice commending us, "I was hungry and you fed me, I was sick and you visited me, I was naked and you clothed me."

Here and Now

To use this story as a way of fore-casting our personal destiny beyond the grave is to miss its urgency for caring for our neighbor here and now. The essence of the story is about our relationship to God, which is measured by our relationship to those in need. The story, in

How do you interpret Jesus' story in relation to social problems? Do you believe the church should be involved in social justice issues? Why or why not? In the story, Jesus says, "All the nations will be gathered before [the Son of Man]." What are the implications of Jesus' teachings for the nations today?

order to be complete, needs the two contrasting behaviors, symbolized by the sheep and the goats. To have spoken only of the sheep (those who are caring) would have overlooked an important fact of life: What happens to us when we do not practice love for our neighbor? That is, the story under-scores that our relationship to our neighbor is a life-and-death matter and that however successful and virtuous our lives are, we will have missed out on life's most profound gifts and we will not even know it.

Not knowing God through acts of caring for our neighbor is the greatest loss of all. The judgment of which this story speaks is not about some future hell but about having lived and never having loved. The story not only models for us faithful behavior, it also holds us account-able, thereby offering us the opportunity to love God by being ever more loving toward our neighbor who is in need.

CLOSING WORSHIP

Sing the hymn "Lord, I Want to Be a Christian." Silently and prayerfully reflect on Matthew 25:31-46. Write on an index card specific needs of specific individuals to which you can respond in a caring way. Keep the card to take home as a reminder of this commitment. Recite the first stanza of the hymn "For the Healing of the Nations" as a closing prayer.

---

[1] From *Weapons of the Spirit*, a film by Pierre Sauvage (1989).

[2] From *Unexpected News: Reading the Bible With Third World Eyes*, by Robert McAfee Brown (Westminster Press, 1984); page 133.

[3] From *Engaging the Powers*, by Walter Wink (Fortress Press, 1992); page 135.

[4] From *Unexpected News: Reading the Bible With a Third World Eye*; page 134.

Session

6

A MINISTRY OF COMPASSION

Luke 4:14-30; 8:40-56; 10:25-37

Contemporary life offers many opportunities to reach out to those who live in poverty or oppression and to those who need hope and healing. Jesus demonstrated in his ministry that the good neighbor is one who reaches across all boundaries to show mercy to others.

GATHERING

Read aloud Luke 4:18-19. Choose a statement from this passage and write a brief statement about what it means to you. Talk about what you wrote with one or two others in the group. Pray the following prayer: "We thank you for Jesus whose ministry is described in these words from the prophet Isaiah. May these words be a light to our own path of faith as we walk the crowded ways of life. Sensitize us to the needs of those we encounter daily, and empower us to join with Jesus in proclaiming to all we meet the good news of God's favor. Amen."

Exploiting the Poor

The exploitation of the poor by the rich is a theme woven throughout history. Here are some examples.

When slavery in the United States ended, many former slaves found work on farms owned by white people. A common arrangement was called "sharecropping" in which black families lived on and worked the land in exchange for a portion of the crops. The black tenant farmers survived by consuming some of the farm products and selling the rest for cash, usually to the landowner, who in turn resold them at a higher price. Some of the white owners were scrupulous and fair, but most of them took advantage of the laborers.

One way this exploitation was carried out was through the company store, a general store operated by the landowner. A tenant farmer, who earned very little cash anyway, would purchase merchandise at the company store on credit. This credit account would accumulate for several months until harvest time. The landowner would then take the cash that he would have paid the tenant for his portion of the crop and deduct that amount from the tenant's debt. Very little cash was left over, consigning the tenant and his family to an endless cycle of poverty. Sharecropping was simply another form of slavery.

> *What stories in the newspaper have you read that describe the plight of the poor or disabled? Some people say that poverty is caused by laziness. What do you say? What do you hear Jesus saying?*

Robbery of the poor is widespread in our own society. One device for this is the establishment of a minimum wage that is far below a living wage. Furthermore, so long as an employee works less than three-quarter time, the employer is not required to provide health and retirement benefits. Consequently, millions of our citizens, merely in order to provide rent and food for their families, are forced to hold down two (and sometimes three) part-time jobs. In those families, children suffer because their parents are stretched thin. This system is designed to provide the corporate owners with exorbitant wealth at the expense of overworked and underpaid employees.

Profiting at the expense of the poor can be documented on the international level. Rich nations impose on poorer nations a system of debt perpetuation that operates on the same principle as the company store. The rich nations make loans to poorer nations; but the debt of the poorer nations is so great that most of the borrowed money is eaten up in interest which, of course, goes back into the coffers of the wealthy nations. Consequently, very little of the total loan is available for the poor countries to use for education, housing, health care, and infrastructure rebuilding. Thus poverty continues indefinitely.

A Vision of Ministry

In that fateful first sermon at Nazareth where his listeners seemed ready to stone him, Jesus declared that God had called him to stand up for the poor precisely because they were victims of the economic system. Luke 4:18-19, which brings together quotations from Isaiah 61:1-2 and 58:6, elegantly summarizes Jesus' understanding of his ministry. It begins with the empowerment of the Spirit and views Jesus' ministry through the lenses of the prophetic tradition and the fulfillment of Scripture.

A radical concept that is described in the Book of Leviticus is that of Jubilee. Leviticus 25:8-12 calls for a period of celebration in the 49th year in which "you shall proclaim liberty throughout the land to all its inhabitants." The intent is that all who have been put in debtor's prison shall be released, which indeed would be "good news to the poor" since only the poor were locked up because of debt. Just as there is to be sabbath rest on the seventh day, there is to be a period of rest for the land on the 49th year (seven times seven). "To demonstrate that God is the ultimate owner of everything, nothing is to be harvested in the seventh year. The natural produce of the land is to feed poor people. . . . Wildlife is to be given a chance to repopulate itself."[1]

The concept is idealistic and probably was too impractical to apply on a permanent basis. Yet it remained a part of the Jewish vision for a communal life centered in God alone and must have shaped Jesus' belief in the kingdom of God. Luke 4:18-19 ends with a reference to "the year of the Lord's favor," that is, a jubilee year.

Jesus' life and ministry cannot be fully understood and appreciated apart from his commitment to the poor and disenfranchised. This is not to say that he was unconcerned for the well-off. Quite the contrary. His ministry to the rich was two-fold.

First, he tried to awaken them to their complicity in promoting poverty through their greed and indifference. "How hard it is for those who have wealth to enter the kingdom of God! Indeed, it is easier for a camel to go through the eye of a needle than for someone who is rich to enter the kingdom of God" (Luke 18:24-25).

> Read Isaiah 58:6; 61:1-2; and Luke 4:18-19. What do these passages say to you about Jesus' understanding of his ministry as Luke presents it?

Second, Jesus wanted to help them become aware of the riches of a life of genuine sharing. On one occasion, a wealthy young man asked Jesus how he might have eternal life. "Jesus, looking at him, loved him and said, 'You lack one thing; go, sell what you own, and give the money to the poor, and you will have treasure in heaven; then come, follow me'" (Mark 10:21).

Heal Me, Lord

Jesus' ministry as a healer is underscored in Luke's story of two healings (8:40-56). The intertwined healing stories demonstrate the power of Jesus over sickness and death. They also demonstrate that compassion overrules the demands of religious ritual.

The woman with the hemorrhage was considered unclean, as was the corpse of Jairus's daughter. Jesus reached across such ritual barriers repeatedly in his healing ministry in order to offer healing, life, and wholeness to the one in need. In Luke 8:50, Jesus reassures Jairus, "Do not fear. Only believe, and she will be saved."

> Read Luke 8:40-56. What, if anything, challenges you in these healing stories? What do these two stories tell us about Jesus' reputation as a healer? about his ministry of compassion?

The Greek word for "believe" is *pisteuō?*, which means to entrust or to have faith as well as to believe. The word is another form of the word translated as "faith" when Jesus tells the woman healed of the hemorrhage, "Daughter, your faith has made you well; go in peace." In both cases, faith, trust, believing, and wholeness are interconnected.

Not only does Jesus heal the woman and Jairus's daughter, he offers reassurance—to the healed woman and to those who surround Jairus's daughter.

Two contemporary healing stories show that Jesus' healing ministry continues today.

The author, poet, and dramatist Maya Angelou tells a dramatic story about her son, Guy. He sustained a broken neck in an automobile accident, and she spent the night before surgery praying. When the doctors came out of surgery, they informed her that Guy would be paralyzed from the neck down. She went in and talked with Guy about it; and he begged her, through tears, to disconnect his life supports because he did not want to live as a quadriplegic.

When the doctors came in to explain the hopelessness of Guy's case, Angelou responded: "I'm not asking you, I'm *telling* you. My son will walk out of this hospital, and I thank God for it—now!"

She contacted friends of various faiths across the country and asked them to pray for Guy's healing. She joined them, praying all night. The next day, a nurse told her that Guy had moved his toes. Angelou went in to see the boy, pulled the blanket off his feet, and saw his toes move. "Thank you, God," she said. "Didn't I ask you for it, and didn't you give it to me?" Months later, the impossible happened: Guy walked out of the hospital.[2]

A critical element in this story is the boy's—and the doctor's—need for hope. The compassion of Christ shone through Angelou's faith, which in turn gave hope to patient and doctors. This same compassion expressed itself in the biblical healing when Jesus said to the woman, "Daughter, your faith has made you well; go in peace" (8:48).

> *What do the healing stories in Luke 8:40-56 offer to those who do not experience a physical cure in spite of their faith and trust in Christ?*

When a loved one is in critical condition, our prayer, of course, is for the kind of healings just described; but we know that does not always happen. This does not mean, however, that God fails to hear and answer our prayers. One quality of God we can always count on is compassion. No matter how serious our medical condition, God never abandons us.

An example of this was in the case of Jim Hardison, an Episcopal clergyman who was diagnosed with brain cancer. Following surgery, he was told he had approximately 12 months to live. Jim, with the support of his wife, Mary, and his three grown children, determined he would make the most of those months by engaging in a healing ministry to other cancer patients. He regularly visited the hospital, taking communion to those who wished it. Sometimes, when he was unable to leave home, he would talk by phone with these patients, offering a prayer for their healing. As the cancer grew, Jim experienced an increased limitation in his vocabulary so that he was often unable to recall words he used regularly.

Read Luke 8:40-56 again. What connections do you make between the stories in Luke and the two contemporary stories of healing? How do you see healing in the contemporary stories? Describe an experience of healing, either your own or one you know about, in which healing may not have involved a physical cure? How did healing happen?

On one occasion, Mary heard Jim praying on the phone with another cancer patient. Unable to recall the word "heal," Jim prayed, "*Repair* us, O Lord, that we may *repair* others."

One evening, when Jim and Mary returned from their church's weekly healing service, the couple sat down and had a time of sharing. Jim said, "I am so grateful for the people who are praying for me to be cured of cancer. I don't want them to stop. But from now on I am praying that, with whomever I meet, I will *know* and *be* the love of God for them."

Jim offered such compassion to others that he was a source of hope and healing, and he continued to do this until his death. In this, Jesus was a model, for as he faced death, in his utter weakness, Jesus reached out in compassion to those around him.

Who Is My Neighbor?

Jesus intended that we, his followers, should continue the ministry for which God had anointed him. The parable of the Good Samaritan is a call to that ministry (Luke 10:25-37). Here is the story of a contemporary Good Samaritan.

The conflict between the Israelis and Palestinians is tragic. In the midst of conflict, an Israeli named Jeff Halper has organized Palestinians and Israelis for the purpose of rebuilding Palestinian homes. Every weekend a group of these workers gathers on the West Bank to construct a home for a Palestinian family. Sometimes the Israeli army will bulldoze these new homes, but Jeff's group will return and rebuild. This non-violent act of working together with traditional enemies is a remarkable example of peacemaking. Jeff occasionally comes to the United States to tell his story and to gain financial support from Christians and other groups. The name of the program is "Raise the Roof." Hundreds of Americans have donated money to this laudable cause.

In Jesus' classic parable of the good Samaritan, he was illustrating what it means to be a good neighbor. The conversation had been initiated by a lawyer who asked Jesus what he must do to inherit eternal life. Jesus quoted ancient Jewish teachings about loving God and neighbor: "And who is my neighbor?" asked the lawyer. Presumably the lawyer hoped to

> *Cite contemporary examples of people who have defied prejudice in order to love their neighbor. What are factors that inhibit us from being good neighbors? What are rewards for being good neighbors? What experiences have you had in trying to be a good neighbor?*

get Jesus entangled in a definition that the lawyer could pick apart. (This would enable the lawyer to continue avoiding the hard work of loving his neighbor on the grounds that that part of the Law had not yet been made clear to him!)

Sidestepping the lawyer's bait, Jesus told a story about three men who came upon a man who had been beaten up and left on the road to die (Luke 10:30-37). The two most religious men, the priest and Levite, "passed by on the other side," while the Samaritan stopped and rendered aid, even taking the victim to an inn and paying for his care. Samaritans and Jews were avowed enemies, yet this Samaritan performed the loving act. "Which of these three men...was the neighbor?" asked Jesus. Cleverly, Jesus had turned the lawyer's question around: not "Who is my neighbor?" but "Whose neighbor am I?" The lawyer answered, "The one who showed him mercy." Jesus said to him, "Go and do likewise" (Luke 10:37).

An Example for Us

Jesus' ministry consistently crossed boundaries in order to express compassion and to offer hope and wholeness. He shows us in his actions as well as in his teaching how we can be compassionate through serving others. As with Jesus, the Spirit of God has descended on us, anointing us to reach out in love and service to our neighbors in need.

CLOSING WORSHIP

Read aloud Luke 4:18-19. Select one or two of the ministries in the Luke passage and write down specific ways in which you are willing to commit yourself to respond to God's call.

Prayer: "Send us forth with your blessing, Lord. Open our eyes to the needs of our daily world, and give us the vision to see your presence in every human being we encounter. We are your servants, Lord; and we depart knowing that your Spirit has already descended upon us to guide us into daily ministry. Thank you for the privilege of being a part of your ministry in the world. Amen."

[1] From *The Book of Leviticus, The New Interpreter's Bible*, (Abingdon Press, 1994); page 1171.

[2] From *Story in the Feminine Face of God*, by Sherry Ruth Anderson and Patricia Hopkins (Bantam Books, 1992); pages 136-39.

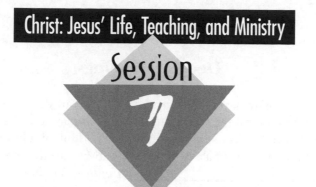

Session 7

HUMILITY AND HOSPITALITY

Luke 14:7-24

Humility and hospitality are key features of Christian life. This session explores the connections between humility and hospitality in order that we might discover ways to view ourselves with humility, to accept graciously the recognition and exteem offered by others, and to value others as we value ourselves.

GATHERING

On newsprint, write "humility" and "hospitality." How does the culture perceive these words? What positive images are associated with them? What negative images? What connections exist between the words?

Prayer: "Thank you, God, for inviting us to this great banquet of life! Forgive the ways in which we take your generosity for granted and fail to recognize that all of life is a gift. Help us to learn from Jesus' example how to show generous hospitality to the people who are part of our daily lives. We know we have much to learn about humility and hospitality, Lord. Thank you for being so patient with us. Amen."

Deeper Meanings

Many of us may have very negative ideas about the meaning of the word *humility*. Our images of a humble person may reflect self-effacing gestures that reveal low self-esteem. We may think of a humble person as something of a doormat. A little exploration into the word family of *humility* may help correct such images. The ancient root word of *humility* means "earth" and includes in its family such words as *humble*, *humus*, *human*, and *homage*.[1] We can say with a certain amount of accuracy that humility nurtures growth in much the same way that humus or rich, vegetative soil, nurtures growth.

> *How do the word histories affect your understanding of the words* humility *and* hospitality?

It is also true that we tend to limit the meaning of the word *hospitality* to the mere expression of courtesy to one's guests. It is certainly the practice of such courtesy, but it is more. It is in the same family as the words *hospital*, *host*, and *guest*.[2] Because it points to the stranger, the guest, and the host, the root suggests reciprocity in the practice of hospitality.

While *humility* and *hospitality* have different meanings, they are interconnected and related as illustrated in the following story.

When Otto transferred, mid-year, into the eighth grade of Lakeside Middle School, he had just moved with his family from his native Germany. His English was passable, but he often had difficulty in making himself understood. The students sometime laughed at his broken English and his occasional misuse of the language.

Seeing himself at a disadvantage, he compensated by working harder than most students and also by keeping a distance from them. This distancing was interpreted by the students as an attitude of superiority, resulting in Otto's being more isolated.

One day in literature class, Otto was having difficulty understanding a story by John Steinbeck because he simply lacked the background. When he asked questions in class for clarification, the questions often sounded stupid to the other students. The other students looked at each other and laughed at Otto. Recognizing Otto's need for help, the teacher asked if someone would volunteer to meet with him after class to help him. There was a long silence, so the teacher asked again. No response. "Well, Otto," she said, "why don't you come by after school today, and you and I can talk about the Steinbeck story?"

"That won't be necessary," Brenda suddenly blurted out. "I'll meet with you, Otto. We can go to the library when school lets out."

"Thank you, Brenda," said the teacher. Otto, obviously surprised by Brenda's thoughtfulness, looked at her and smiled broadly.

As the class was filing out, several students made snide remarks to Brenda. Some hinted that she was trying to get brownie points from the teacher; others put her down for siding with the "foreigner." The jabs hurt Brenda's feelings, but she did not let them stand in the way of keeping her promise.

> Who are the Ottos in your experience? Who are the Brendas? What situations in your life are similar to this one? How does Brenda's response demonstrate hospitality? humility? How can we recognize the importance of self-esteem while avoiding self-centeredness? How can we affirm individual worth while maintaining community?

Among adolescents, being cool and one of the in-crowd have always been cherished values. When Brenda volunteered to help someone who was not particularly popular in class, she broke the exclusivity code. This was, on her part, a deed of courage and an act of humility.

Our natural tendency is to put ourselves first, and this stands in the way of our living in community. Brenda set an example for the class by taking a risk to include Otto, thereby enabling the class to be more of a community for this newcomer.

God's Vision for Human Society (Luke 14:7-24)

Luke's Gospel recounts a set of mealtime teachings about true hospitality and the values of humility as expressions of life in God's kingdom. Jesus is eating a meal on the sabbath at the home of a leader of the Pharisees. Pharisees expressed their awareness of God's grace and their devotion to God by giving their lives to following the letter of the Law in every aspect of life. Jesus' teachings pointed to the heart of the Law as God originally intended it. During the meal, he heals a man with dropsy and thus prioritizes attending to human need over sabbath observances (Luke 14:1-6). This healing sets the stage for a series of teachings in which he challenges those present to look again at God's vision for human society and honor.

Read Luke 14:7-11. Read also Luke 13:30; 18:14; and Matthew 18:4; 23:12. What challenges you about this teaching? What do you think Jesus is saying to the others at the dinner? How does the teaching speak to social customs in the contemporary world?

Jesus notices guests choosing places of honor, which gives rise to a practical observation. If you choose the best seat, the host might ask you to move in order to make space for a more honored guest. Take the lowest seat, therefore, and it is likely that you will be invited to take a more important seat (Proverbs 25:6-7).

The section culminates with the well-known teaching about humility: "For all who exalt themselves will be humbled, and those who humble themselves will be exalted" (Luke 14:11. See also Matthew 18:4; 23:12; Luke 13:30; 18:14.) As is so characteristic of Jesus, he points beyond the moment to a way of life that is a reversal of the social standards of the day, the way of life in God's kingdom. Honor can neither be seized nor be achieved by feigned humility. True honor is a gift.

Who's on Your Guest List?

After addressing the action of the guests, Jesus speaks to the host. In the social structures of the day, the host may choose or invite guests in order to achieve honor. The core motivation is similar to that of the guests who choose the seat of honor. Jesus reverses the common social rule.

"When you give a luncheon or a dinner, do not invite your friends or your brothers or your relatives or rich neighbors, in case they may invite you in return, and you would be repaid. But when you give a banquet, invite the poor, the crippled, the lame, and the blind. And you will be blessed, because they cannot repay you, for you will be repaid at the resurrection of the righteous" (Luke 14:12-14).

Why this concern with humility and with ways to achieve honor? As always, Jesus points beyond the immediate context to life in God's kingdom, life lived God's ways. True humility recognizes God as the source of all. The gift of God's honor is far greater than any honor we try to carve out for ourselves as "guests" and "hosts" in our world.

R.S.V.P.

The third parable at the meal setting, Luke 14:15-24, is the parable of the great banquet. The parable focuses on the responses of the invited guests and the reaction of the host. It further develops Jesus' teachings about humility and hospitality as features of life in God's kingdom, and in addition, it adds a sharp criticism by showing the excuses made to the host for not attending the banquet. In each case, the R.S.V.P. is "No, thank you; and here's why ..." The host of this great banquet is, in effect, snubbed by those initially invited. In the end it is the social outcast—those who are poor, crippled, blind, and lame—who will dine with the host.

> *Read aloud Luke 14:15-24. If you have time, develop a skit based on this parable. What do you think of the excuses offered to the host? What do you make of the snubbed host's response? Given the context in which Jesus tells the parable, a meal at the home of a Pharisee, what do you think Jesus might be saying about God's kingdom? How do you think those who heard the parable might have responded to it?*

God's Kingdom Includes All

The teachings that Jesus offers to the guests and the host at the dinner also embrace inclusiveness, a subject that has been the source of tension and controversy since the church's beginning. In its earliest days, there were Jewish Christians, such as Peter, who believed that Jews and Gentiles should eat at separate tables. Peter was not a bigot; he was just abiding by the Torah's stand on holiness that he had been taught since childhood.

However, one day Peter, while asleep, had a vision in which he heard the voice of God saying to him, "What God has made clean, you must not call profane" (Acts 10:15), meaning that Jews and Gentiles—and all persons—are children of God; and all are of equal worth. When the subject came up in the church in Galatia, Paul wrote a strongly-worded letter scolding the Galatians for exalting the Law over grace, thereby creating artificial divisions within the body of Christ. The purpose of Christ's death was to overcome these divisions and to unify all humanity. Paul wrote: "There is no longer Jew or Greek, there is no longer slave or free, there is no longer male and female; for all of you are one in Christ Jesus" (Galatians 3:28).

Through the centuries, the church has been conflicted over the subject of inclusiveness. The saying that "eleven o'clock on Sunday morning is the most segregated hour of the week" is a cliché that continues to be true even after the end of slavery and the changes brought about by the civil rights movement. Women, whose work in the church has been so essential, were finally admitted into the ordained ministry of our denomination just decades ago. Discrimination against persons based on sexual orientation continues to be a source of deep pain for those who are not fully accepted; and the most persistent source of divisiveness over the centuries has been classism, wherein the church has imitated society's communal standards, which are mostly dictated by wealth.

> *Have you ever experienced discrimination in the church because of your skin color, gender, sexual orientation, or economic status? Do you know others who have? What does discrimination do to a person? Where have you noted the standards of Jesus to be in conflict with the practices of the church? How do you think these contradictions should be resolved?*

The Last Shall Be First

Flannery O'Connor's short story "Revelation" is an engaging tale about a woman who, through painful experience, comes to learn the meaning of humility, hospitality, and inclusiveness in God's kingdom.

Mrs. Turpin is a woman who takes great pride in being hard-working and, according to her standards, righteous. One day while in the doctor's waiting room, she is talking pompously about herself when a disturbed teenage girl, who cannot stand to hear her any longer, suddenly throws a book at Mrs. Turpin and then tackles her to the floor. Medical personnel pull the girl off of Mrs. Turpin and take her away but not before the girl shouts, "Go back to hell where you came from, you old wart hog."

Mrs. Turpin is so distressed by this attack that she ponders it day and night, trying to make sense of it. Being a very religious person, she believes that God may have been sending her a message but she has difficulty believing she deserved it. She had always entertained fantasies about her righteousness and had frequently imagined, at the final judgment, seeing a line of saints traipsing across the sky toward heaven, with her and her husband near the front of the crowd. At the end would be black people, followed by poor whites.

Then one day, after the traumatic experience in the doctor's office, she had that vision again; but this time it was quite different. The heavenward procession was the same as before, except the order was completely reversed. Poor whites and black people were at the head, and at the very end were the tribe of people that included her and her husband. "She could see by their shocked and altered faces that even their virtues were being burned away."[3]

In the parable of the great banquet (Luke 14:15-24), there is a tension between the generous host who welcomes anyone and everyone, regardless of their status, and the privileged invitees who had better things to do than gather with this crowd. Jesus' genuine friendship with outcasts represents God's inclusiveness of everyone in the Kingdom's fellowship, a model of true hospitality. Getting beyond our tendency to be exclusive requires a humility that is modeled so well by Jesus.

> *What experiences have you had in which a negative outlook toward some person or group of people has undergone transformation? Identify one person in your church fellowship with whom you have difficulty relating. How might the parable or the O'Connor story help you to see God at work in that relationship?*

In the Flannery O'Connor story, Mrs. Turpin experienced a spiritual earthquake that enabled her to view herself and her world from God's perspective, and it is obvious that she recognized the painful judgment as a gift of divine grace. Jesus' intention in telling the disturbing parable in Luke 14 is that we who have ears to hear will recognize that God is offering us the possibility of a world of relationships with all people, including those we scorn and reject. Such a world is far richer than a world we might fashion according to our own narrow standards. The best news in all this is that the gift is ours now, if we have the grace to accept it.

Living God's Way

Our study together has been a journey with Jesus. Perhaps for you ths odyssey began when you first came to know Jesus as a child in Sunday school. Maybe the journey began more recently. In either case, I hope that the remarkable life of Jesus Christ—shown in his life, teaching, and ministry—continues to be enriching and transforming for you. His life, teaching, and ministry illuminate what it means to live as God intends, that is, to live now and always in God's kingdom.

CLOSING WORSHIP

Sing or read the words to the hymn "In Christ There Is No East or West."

Pray silently about what you have learned about the life, teaching, and ministry of Jesus. Close the session by praying the Lord's Prayer.

---

[1] From *The New American Heritage Dictionary of the English Language*, Third Edition (Houghton Mifflin Company, 1992); page 2101.

[2] From *The New American Heritage Dictionary of the English Language*; page 2105.

[3] From *The Complete Stories*, by Flannery O'Connor (Farrar, Straus, Giroux, 1984); pages 488-509.

Appendix

Background Scriptures for
"Christ: Jesus' Life, Teaching, and Ministry"

Mark 1:4-13	Matthew 13:1-23
Mark 2:1-12	Matthew 18:21-35
Mark 14:53-65	Matthew 25:31-46
Mark 15:1-5	Luke 4:14-30
Mark 16:1-8	Luke 8:40-56
Mark 5:1-16	Luke 10:25-37
Mark 6:1-18	Luke 14:7-24

The Committee on the Uniform Series

The Committee on the Uniform Series (CUS) is made up of persons appointed by their respective denominations, which, although differing in certain elements of faith and polity, hold a common faith in Jesus Christ, the Son of God, as Lord and Savior, whose saving gospel is to be taught to all humankind. CUS has about 70 members who represent 19 protestant denominations in the US and Canada, who work together to develop the International Bible Lessons for Christian Teaching. A team from this committee develops the cycles of scriptures and themes that form the backbone of the Bible lesson development guides. The cycles present a balance between Old and New Testaments, although the weight is on the latter. Cycles through 2016 are organized around the following themes: creation, call, covenant, Christ, community, commitment, God, hope, worship, tradition, faith, and justice.

—MARVIN CROPSEY,
Chair, Committee on the Uniform Series

Other Bible Study Resources

If your group would like to study other short-term small-group resources, we recommend:

The Jesus Collection—a series of books about the life, teachings, and ministry of Jesus Christ, each of which invites the reader into renewal and commitment.

The Life and Letters of Paul Series—Historical, archaeological, and geographic data interwoven into a fascinating study of Paul's epistles. Each book takes an in-depth look at particular aspects of Paul's ministry as illuminated in his letters.

The FaithQuestions series—Offers studies of issues in theology, ethics, missions, biblical interpretation, and church history. Designed for adults who seek a deeper engagement with the Christian faith and with scripture.

If your group would like to explore a long-term Bible study, we recommend:

Adult Bible Study—Published quarterly. Thirteen lessons per quarter. Bible study resources based on the International Lesson Series, also known as the Uniform Series

Genesis to Revelation—a comprehensive study based on the New International Version of the Bible. Twenty-four volumes. Thirteen sessions per volume.

Journey Through the Bible—a comprehensive study based on the New Revised Standard Version of the Bible. Sixteen Volumes. Thirteen sessions per volume.

DISCIPLE Bible Study—a 34-week foundation study of the Bible in which participants learn how to become more effective disciples through Bible study.